JOHANNES ITTEN

DESIGN AND FORM

The Basic Course at the Bauhaus

Translated by John Maass

REINHOLD PUBLISHING CORPORATION · NEW YORK

© 1963   Otto Maier Verlag Ravensburg, Germany
Printed in Ravensburg, Germany

Originally published in Germany under the title:
„Mein Vorkurs am Bauhaus. Gestaltungs- und Formenlehre"

English Translation © 1964 by Reinhold Publishing Corporation

Library of Congress Catalog Card Number 63-19225

CONTENTS

Teaching cannot be repeated in its most valuable moments — when we succeed in touching a student's innermost core and striking a spiritual light.

This description of my teaching seems to me poor compared with what actually happened. The tone, the rhythm, the sequence of words, place and time, the mood of the students, and all the other circumstances which make for a vital atmosphere cannot be reproduced; yet it is the ineffable which helps form a climate of creativity. My teaching was intuitive finding. My own emotion gave me the power which produced the student's readiness to learn. To teach out of inner enthusiasm is the opposite of a mere pre-planned method of instruction.

My best students are those who found new ways through their own intuition. Mere outward imitation and repetition of my procedure is without sparking power. Yet I am well aware that my teaching did not always embody something new; it was also a revival of what had been the fundamentals for artists of the past.

I owe my first educational insights to the young open-minded director of a teachers' college. He showed me that children in their natural simplicity can invent amazingly original drawings, stories, and songs. When I first taught in 1908 at the elementary school of a Swiss village, I tried to avoid anything which would disturb the children's naïveté. Almost instinctively I realized that all criticism and corrections offend and destroy self-confidence, while encouragement and recognition further the growth of abilities.

After a year of teaching, the atmosphere in class was homelike, tender, and sensitive. When the school inspector came, he grabbed some notebooks from a stack and addressed me furiously: "Don't you know that correcting essays is part of the teacher's job?"

"I believe that every correction in an essay has an offensive effect which destroys the child's natural storytelling," I replied. "Then what about spelling?" he demanded. "I read the essays and note the mistakes," I explained. "When I return the notebooks these mistakes are discussed with the entire class; the words are written on the blackboard, and the pupils enter them alphabetically in their notebooks. After a few weeks we have a dictation test. So the pupils learn to spell hundreds of words correctly in a year."

In no human activity is talent as decisive as in the field of education. Only the talented educator — I mean talented for education — will respect and guard the indescribable wonder of humanity in every child of man. Respect for human beings is the beginning and the end of all education. Education is a bold venture, especially art education, which deals with man's creativity.

Knowledge of human nature — intuitive knowledge — seems to me an essential talent for the true educator; for he should be able to recognize and develop the natural abilities and temperaments of his students.

Teachers who have studied only the methods of imparting fixed curricula to students are like pill sellers filling prescriptions, not like doctors.

When I first studied art in Geneva in 1910, art academies everywhere instructed in a medieval manner. The professors showed the students how they worked, and the students imitated the teachers. Those who imitated best were considered prize pupils. Disappointed, I returned to the University of Berne to continue my training as a high school teacher.

A trip from Berne to Holland and a visit to the Sonderbund Exhibition in Cologne led me to the renewed decision to give up the teaching profession and to become a painter. I now believed that I knew what I wanted to learn, and I went to Geneva for a second time. In a course under Professor Gilliard I learned something decisive: he introduced me to the geometric elements of form and their contrasts.

From 1913 to 1916 I was a student of Adolf Hölzel in Stuttgart. Besides pictorial composition we studied above all the fundamentals of color.

In his lectures, Hölzel explained the pictorial constructions of the old masters and their use of light and dark. Hölzel's whole effort consisted of exploring and teaching the means of design. As a teacher he was receptive to everything new. Among his students I met Ida Kerkovius, Oskar Schlemmer, and Willy Baumeister. In spite of the terrible events of the war, we carried on discussions about the artistic problems of Cubism and Futurism. In 1915-16 I worked on pictorial compositions of geometric abstract forms and mounted natural materials. Hölzel sent me my first students to enable me to make a living. At first, my own work was strongly reflected in my teaching, but through the students' many questions, problems of art education came into focus for me.

In 1916 I moved to Vienna at the invitation of a girl student. The war was still on, and the city was full of somber tensions. To enable me to paint, I again tried to earn my living by teaching. The number of my students soon grew, and I was able to set them new tasks.

We worked on geometric and rhythmic forms, problems of proportion and expressive pictorial composition. Assignments with textures and subjective forms were something new. Besides the study of polar contrasts, exercises for the relaxation and concentration of the students brought amazing successes. I recognized creative automatism as one of the most important factors in art. I myself worked on geometric-abstract pictures which were based on careful pictorial constructions.

In the summer of 1919, Alma Mahler-Gropius, who was very much interested in my painting and teaching, invited me to a talk with her husband Walter Gropius; he had been appointed to direct the State Bauhaus in Weimar. After Gropius had seen my work and that of my students, he proposed that I come to Weimar as a teacher at the Bauhaus.

I was particularly attracted by the studios and workshops and the fact that the Bauhaus was still empty so that the new could be built without much tearing down of the old. Gerhard Marcks and Lyonel Feininger, the teachers appointed by Walter Gropius up to that time, were already there. The aims and ways of the Bauhaus, publicized through a manifesto by Walter Gropius, were still little known in 1919. This manifesto read:

"The ultimate aim of all design activity is the building... Architects, sculptors, painters, we all must go back to handicraft... There is no essential difference between artist and craftsman, the artist is a heightened craftsman ... The foundation of craftsmanship is, however, indispensible for every artist. There is the fountainhead of creative design."

Fourteen of my Vienna students, namely K. Auböck, J. Breuer, M. Cyrenius, F. Dicker, C. Lipovec, V. Neumann, O. Okuniewska, G. Pap, F. Probst, F. Singer, F. Skala, N. Slutzky, M. Tery-Adler and A. Wotiz, followed me to Weimar in the summer of 1919 and formed the nucleus of the first course at the Bauhaus.

For the winter semester 1919–1920, younger and older students from different parts of Germany and with quite diverse educational backgrounds had also registered. Most of them had attended the usual arts and crafts schools and academies. The work which they submitted for admission to the Bauhaus did not reveal their individuality. It was difficult to form a judgment about the students' talent and character.

With my students in Vienna I had discovered that it is possible to awaken slumbering talent for art and to intensify individual originality. I therefore proposed to Walter Gropius that all students who showed an interest in art should be admitted provisionally for one semester. We called this trial semester the "Basic Course." The name Basic Course therefore originally implied neither special subject matter nor a novel method of teaching. I took over direction of the Basic Course in the fall of 1919. Walter Gropius generously gave me complete freedom with the structure and theme of the course.

Three tasks were set for me in the Basic Course:

1. To free the creative powers and thereby the art talents of the students. Their own experiences and perceptions were to lead to genuine work. The students were to free themselves gradually from dead conventions and to take courage for work of their own.

2. To make the students' choice of career easier. Here the exercises with materials and textures proved a valuable aid. In a short time each student found out which materials appealed most to him; whether wood, metal, glass, stone, clay or yarn best stimulated him to creative activity. Unfortunately, at that time we lacked a workshop for the Basic Course in which all fundamental skills, such as planing, filing, sawing, bending, glueing, and soldering, could be practiced.

3. To convey to the students the fundamental principles of design for their future careers. The laws of form and color opened the objective world to the students. In the course of the work the objective and subjective problems of form and color were integrated in many ways.

The Basic Course was to last one semester. After successful completion of the Basic Course the students were to learn a craft in the workshops of the Bauhaus, and at the same time they were to be trained for future cooperation with industry. Fig. 1 shows the curriculum of the Bauhaus in 1923.

In teaching the means of design it seemed important to me to appeal to diverse individual temperaments and talents. This alone makes for a creative atmosphere which encourages original work. The work should be "genuine." The student should gain natural self-confidence and eventually find his profession. People of various talents react quite differently to the elements of design and accordingly develop in different ways. Some are attracted to light-dark, others to form, rhythm, color, proportions and constructions, texture, spatial directions or volume. So I could see a student as a light-dark type or a rhythmic type or as a metal, wood or glass type.

These types are, however, seldom one-dimensional; usually individuality is determined by talents in several directions. I accomplished the unlocking of individual power through a definite way of teaching the means of design.

First, imagination and creative ability must be freed and strengthened. When this is accomplished, technical-practical requirements can be brought in and finally also economic considerations of the market. Young people who start with market research and practical-technical work in mind seldom feel like searching for something really new.

If new ideas are to take the shape of art, it is necessary to prepare and coordinate physical, sensual, spiritual, and intellectual forces and abilities. This insight largely determined the subject and method of my Bauhaus teaching. The task was to build the whole man as a creative being, a program which I also championed again and again in the faculty council.

The post-war political and economic insecurity was very detrimental to our work. Many students were poor and starved into an uncertain future. Studios were available but they were unheated. At first, there were neither tables nor chairs in the classrooms; the students worked squatting on the floor. So I taught only one morning a week during this first winter of 1919 – 1920. For the rest of the time the students worked on the assignments alone and without corrections in their living quarters. This "being on one's own" was not without importance for "finding oneself." Stuffing students with alien knowledge and a lack of time for contemplation hinder individual growth.

When the first Basic Course ended in the spring of 1920, nobody took care of the students who were supposed to enter the workshops; it was up to me to give them work. So I made the students test the fundamental principles of the Basic Course by applying them to objects. Fig. 41 shows the exercise of carving textures, and Fig. 113 is a chest which was made with individually textured surfaces. The stone (Fig. 114), the metalwork of the door lock (Fig. 75), and the cans (Figs. 115, 116, 117) were also produced as assignments following my Basic Course. The Bauhaus had no class in architecture. Walter Gropius, who was the only architect at the Bauhaus, had no time to teach, as he was fully occupied with organizational problems and private commissions. At that time I started with all the students who had no one to teach them. Paul Klee, Georg Muche and Oskar Schlemmer were called to the Bauhaus at my suggestion. The "faculty council" was only complete in the summer of 1921, and the workshops got their masters.

10

The terrible events and shattering losses of the war had brought chaos and confusion in all fields. Among the students there were endless discussions and eager searching for a new mental attitude. My attention was drawn to Spengler's book, "The Decline of the West." I became conscious that our scientific-technical civilization had come to a critical point. The slogans "Back to Handicraft" or "Unity of Art and Technology" did not seem to me to solve the problems.

I studied oriental philosophy and concerned myself with Persian Mazdaism and Early Christianity. Thus I realized that our outward-directed scientific research and technology must be balanced by inward-directed thought and forces of the soul.

Georg Muche had come to similar conclusions through his war experiences, and we worked in friendly cooperation. We sought the foundations of a new way of life for ourselves and our work. At that time we were ridiculed because we did breathing and concentration exercises. Today the study of oriental philosophy is widespread and many people practice yoga.

These first Weimar years are wrongly described as the romantic period of the Bauhaus. In my opinion, these were the years of universal interests. Certainly mistakes were made in the exuberance of feverish search and practice. We all lacked a great teacher who could have guided us through the ebullient confusion.

It is not only a religious custom to start instruction with a prayer or a song, but it also serves to concentrate the students' wandering thoughts. At the start of the morning I brought my classes to mental and physical readiness for intensive work through relaxing, breathing, and concentrating exercises. The training of the body as an instrument of the mind is of the greatest importance for creative man.

How can the hand express a characteristic emotion through a line when hand and arm are cramped? The fingers, the hand, the arm, the whole body can be awakened through relaxing, strengthening, and sensitizing exercises.

The relaxation of the body can be accomplished in three ways: First, through movements of the arms and legs, through bending and turning the entire body with special attention to the mobility of the spine.

The second approach is to hold the body completely still, standing, sitting or reclining, and to relax part after part through mental concentration. The internal muscles, particularly the important diaphragm, can be relaxed only in this way.

The third method of relaxing, balancing, and harmonizing the body is the use of tone vibration. At first, the students must practice the formation of tones; they must learn where the tones vibrate in the body. The hummed tone must be intensive even when it is sounded softly. A tone filled with the powers of the heart can accomplish wonders.

Besides relaxation, breathing is of the greatest importance. As we breathe, so do we think and so is the rhythm of our daily life. People of great, successful accomplishments always have a quiet, slow and deep breath. Shortwinded people are hasty and greedy in thought and action. Through exercises I tried to educate the students to breathe quietly and deeply.

All these exercises have the right effect only when they are done with mental concentration. New students first participated in these morning exercises with some surprise and inner resistance, but after a few days most of them joined with enthusiasm (Fig. 6). I supplemented the relaxing, tone, and breathing exercises with short talks on general topics of practical life. This produced the essential receptivity in class, and I was able to begin work on the means of design.

In working out these themes I always held to the three-step principle: experience — perception — ability.

First I tried to evoke a vivid feeling for the theme through visual experience; next followed the intellectual explaining and comprehending, and only then the execution of the task. Common exercises in drawing always introduced the theme of the day. Paul Klee, who visited the Bauhaus in January, 1921, for his orientation, came unexpectedly into my Basic Course while we were doing rhythmic form exercises. In a letter to his wife of January 16th, 1921, he wrote in a slightly ironical manner: "...After Itten has taken a few walks, he steers towards an easel on which stands a drawing board with layers of scratch paper. He grabs a charcoal; his body rallies as if he were charging himself with electricity, and then he suddenly attacks twice. We see two energetic strokes, vertical and parallel || on the first scratch sheet; the students are asked to do the same. The master checks the work; he makes some of them demonstrate individually; he checks the posture. Then he commands, and, beating time later, he makes them all do the same exercises standing up. This seems to be intended as a kind of body massage to train the machine for emotional functioning. In a similar manner new elementary forms like ⌀ and others are demonstrated and copied, for example ⊗ and 𝍌 with repeated comments about the why, the expression, etc.

"Then he tells something of the wind, makes some of them stand up and assume the expression of their feelings in wind and storm. He then gives the assignment: representation of a storm. He allows about ten minutes, then checks the results and holds a critique. After the critique, work continues. One sheet after another is ripped off and falls to the floor. Some students work with such force that they squander several sheets at once. Finally, after everybody is somewhat tired, he makes the students of the Basic Course take the assignment home for further practice..."

The foundation of my design teaching was the general theory of contrast. Light and dark, material and texture studies, form and color theory, rhythm and expressive forms were discussed and presented in their contrasting effects. Finding and enumerating the various possibilities of contrast was always one of the most exciting lessons because the students realized that a whole new world was opening up for them. Such contrasts are:

Large-small, long-short, broad-narrow, thick-thin, black-white, much-little, straight-bent, pointed-blunt, horizontal-vertical, diagonal-circular, high-low, plane-line, plane-volume, line-volume, smooth-rough, hard-soft, still-moving, light-heavy, transparent-opaque, steady-intermittent, fluid-solid, sweet-sour, strong-weak, loud-soft, plus the seven color contrasts. All these contrasts had to be worked out singly and in combinations (Figs. 2, 3, 4, 5).

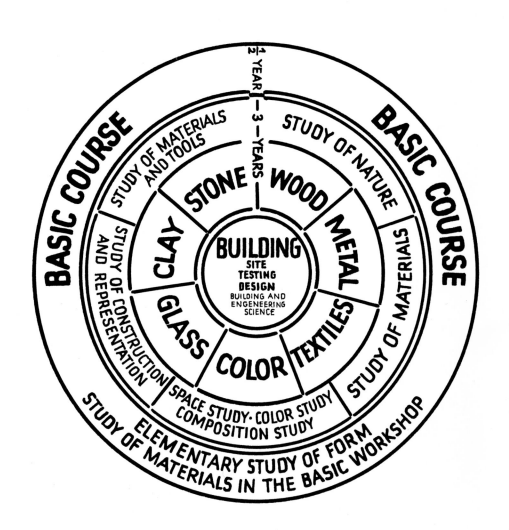

1 Diagram of the Bauhaus curriculum, published 1923.

point   line   plane   volume

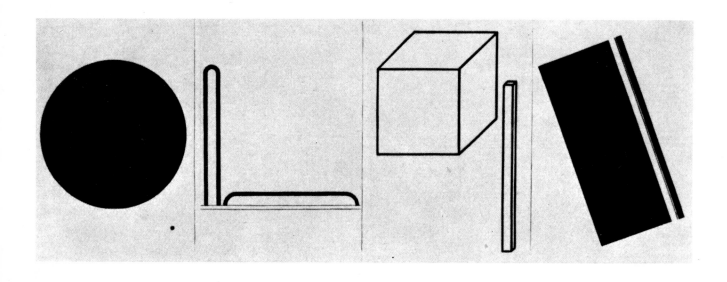

large-small   high-low   thick-thin   broad-narrow

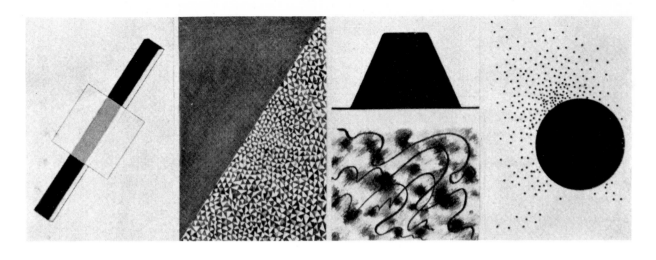

transparent-opaque smooth-rough rest-motion much-little

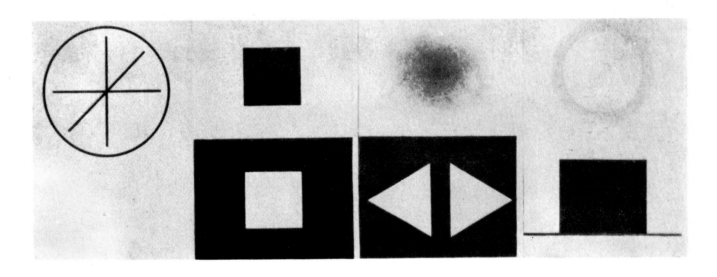

directional contrasts light-dark soft-hard light-heavy

15

6 Morning exercises on the roof of the Itten School Berlin, 1931.

The students had to study the contrasts in three ways: to experience sensuously, to objectify rationally, to realize as a synthesis.

Contrasts like white-black, large-small, cold-warm are specially stressed points in the world of contrasts. As the life and beauty of our earth unfold in the regions between the North Pole and the South Pole, so the gradations between the poles of contrast contain the life and beauty of the worlds of contrast. With the light-dark contrast the artistic possibilities lie in the many tone steps and color values between black and white. Black and white are turning points and not terminals of the light-dark character. The poles of all other contrasts have the same significance; therefore the possibilities of contrasting are infinite.

Adolf Hölzel's penetrating lectures in Stuttgart had shown me the significance of studying the old masters. To know the work of the old masters is useful. It sharpens the consciousness of order and structure in the picture plane and the feeling for rhythm and texture. This study can be hindering and harmful only when we do not control ourselves carefully and fall into academic imitation. After working with form, rhythm, and color fundamentals, I always made the students analyze corresponding works of the old masters to show how they had solved the same problems.

When a pianist seeks to experience a piece at the first playing, he cannot strive to play every note and measure as prescribed by the composer, but must try to grasp the composition as a general whole. Only after many laborious studies of details can he arrive at a faithful rendition. Thus I made the students interpret a black-and-white slide of Grünewald's crucifixion after they had worked on the problems of expressive forms. Like the pianist, the students had to reproduce sensitively how the tragedy of the event was expressed in the picture.

On the occasion of an analysis hour in 1923, Walter Gropius remarked that he could no longer be responsible to the government for my teaching practices. Without further argument I decided to leave the Bauhaus. In 1926 I founded my own art school in Berlin. Painters, graphic artists, architects, and photographers came for a training period of two to three years, and I was able to introduce them to the general study of design more deeply than had been possible in my Basic Course semester at the Bauhaus in Weimar.

In 1931 the velvet and silk industry in Krefeld entrusted me with the establishment of a school for textile designers. For two years I directed both the Berlin and Krefeld schools. In Krefeld it was necessary to meet the requirements of an industrial school, adding technical training to the general art education for designers.

Under Nazi pressure I closed my own school in Berlin. Even the great successes of the state school in Krefeld did not protect it from attacks. The ultimatum to acquire German citizenship was unacceptable to me, and I left Krefeld.

Six months later, I was able to take over the direction of the Arts and Crafts Museum and School in Zurich, and, in 1942, also of the Textile School of the Zurich silk industry. At both schools I taught only half a day a week, as I had many organizational and administrative responsibilities.

The book shows students' work of many years, from my school in Vienna, the Bauhaus in Weimar, the Itten School in Berlin, The Pattern Design School in Krefeld, and the Arts and Crafts School and the Textile Trade School in Zurich.

At the 1923 Bauhaus Exhibition in Weimar, the work of the Basic Course was widely represented. However, the various Bauhaus books were published without my collaboration; unfortunately, the comments on the illustrations from my Basic Course are often misleading or incomplete.

Many works in this book are from my Berlin School; this does not mean that these and similar assignments were not also given in Vienna, Weimar, Krefeld, and Zurich.

My "Diary," produced in 1930 at the Berlin school, is handwritten with many drawings and illustrations; it deals with problems of form and color which I faced as a painter and teacher.

In the book "The Art of Color" (1961) I have presented my color theory. This subject is therefore only outlined in the present book.

This book is not intended to provide a systematic curriculum and sequence of instruction to be imitated. It attempts to convey the essence of my teaching.

With the following saying of Lao-tse, I opened the first students' exhibition in 1918:
"Thirty spokes meet at the hub,
But the void within them creates the essence of the wheel.
Clay forms pots,
But the void within creates the essence of the pot.
Walls with windows and doors make the house,
But the void within them creates the essence of the house.
Fundamentally:
The material contains utility,
The immaterial contains essence."

The contrast between light and dark is one of the most expressive and important means of design for the artist. The students must learn from the start that contrast effects are relative. A line seems long or short as it is related to a shorter or longer line. In a pictorial composition a large dark form becomes more significant if it is opposed by a small light form. A gray tone appears light or dark as we compare it with a darker or lighter tone.

When we want to design with a certain contrast, we must pay attention to this relativity. Contrasting elements should be chosen so that a clear expression is formed.

As an introductory assignment for the study of the light-dark contrast I asked for the representation of a white and a black circle. The students quickly grasped that the outline of a circle drawn on white paper does not define the circle as white. Only when it is surrounded by a more or less dark tone does the circle appear white (Fig. 7).

It is also instructive for students to investigate how dark the surrounding tone must be to make the circle appear white. They experience that a light, delicate gray tone is already sufficient.

In this book I limit myself to the character of light-dark and its representation from white to black. The problems of colored light and dark are thoroughly presented in my color theory. Before assigning exact, intellectual-constructive exercises, themes should be given which can be solved through free feeling and imagination (Fig. 9). For these black and white effects India ink or soft charcoal are useful because they react to the slightest sensation. Another assignment consists of representing white cups, black plates, and a white egg (Fig. 10). Other themes might be black and white spotted chickens or cats, white laundry, or a snowscape with dark fir trees.

Most students find it difficult to perceive many different light and dark tones and to render them cleanly and distinctly. Tone scales must be worked out to improve this seeing and rendering (Fig. 11). I have had interested and gifted students who were able to make visible up to 44 tone gradations between black and white.

The light-dark chords (Figs. 12, 13) show that not only single different values are essential but also the harmony of tones.

Fig. 14 is a difficult problem in composition because areas of different sizes are to have different tone strengths. When representing given concrete forms, the students must direct their entire attention to the contrasts of tone values. Pictures can be analyzed to heighten the feeling for different tone values. Fig. 15 is such a study after Goya. The picture is divided into squares to make the students observe closely every part of the picture. The light-dark contrast is the natural design medium for light and shadow and for three-dimensional forms. It has a meaningful application in nature study. Note that compositions which are based mainly on the effect of light-dark should not be started with outlines; the extent and harmony of spots and masses are determined by the intensity of the light and dark power. Light and dark spots and masses have effects entirely different from those of outlines.

Dark forms are effective on light ground and light forms on dark ground. A light and a dark plane can also be set against one another in one picture. Such a combination is called "reversal" (Fig. 20).

To deepen feeling for tone values I had the students compose non-objective spots in different tonalities. When such works of a whole class are put side by side, the students themselves can easily distinguish the better solutions.

To recognize the possibilities of psychological expression in tone values, the students must solve problems developed from free imagination such as:

Tree in frost
Storm
Dusk
Under the street lamp

In analyzing light-dark values, their compositional and expressive possibilities in old and new masterworks are shown by the use and significance of light-dark in painting. The artist's temperament determines whether he applies light-dark constructively in a clearly visible order, whether it is the purely optical representation of light and shadow, or whether it serves as an emotional quality of expression.

Great masters demonstrate different applications of light and dark. For example, Giotto (Figs. 27–28) and the Master of the Virgo inter Virgines (Fig. 124) have used light and dark as a constructive element of pictorial architecture.

7 White and black circles. Weimar, 1919. F. Dicker.

8 Light-dark variations on a blossom. Berlin, 1926. G. Locher.

9 The assignment, "High white mountain, black fir trees, small white house, green meadows with black and white cows," was given at the beginning of the course to call the students' attention to contrast effects. The contrasts, high-low, large-small and light-dark, are observed and meaningfully used in the composition. Berlin, 1926. U. Klemm.

10 White cups, black plates and a white egg. Berlin, 1931. L. Müller.

11 The first attempts to make a tone value scale between black and white yield only a few unclean tones. Through practice the tones become cleaner, and perception rises to an average number of 20 tone steps. The tones must not be separated by white or black lines; each step must be a single clear tone.

12 Light-dark chord of equal areas.

13 Light-dark chord of different proportions.

14 Areas of different size and tone values are arranged in a balanced composition.

15 Light-dark analysis after Goya's painting "The Duchess of Alba." The picture is geometrized in order to lead the student to a conscious analysis of the entire picture plane. They were not asked to draw the objective forms but to present the main tone values in a simplified way. Berlin, 1931.

16 Light-dark study from nature. Simple objects were posed; after freely choosing objects, the students had to compose a still life. The task is to translate colored planes into light and dark values. The design dispenses with three-dimensional modelling so that the student gains an exact mental image of the characteristic forms.
Berlin, 1930. Molenaar.

17 Geometrized natural forms are composed as a light-dark picture with black, white and gray tones. Berlin, 1930.

18 Drawing of a cluster of blossoms with clearly placed tone values.
Berlin, 1931. S. Bauermeister.

19 Study of a hortensia from nature. Inclusion of the background in the design produces a clear effect of the plant's light blossoms and dark leaves. Krefeld, 1934. H. Funkel.

20 Fall bouquet. The composition shows the placement of light spots on the dark plane and dark spots on the light plane. The spots were done without drawing outlines. The unity of the picture is achieved by the multiplicity of small spots.
Vienna, 1918. E. Anbelang.

21 Horses as a light-dark study. Three-dimensional forms contrast with linear elements. Berlin, 1929. B. von Graefe.

22 Portrait study in light-dark modulations. Berlin, 1932.

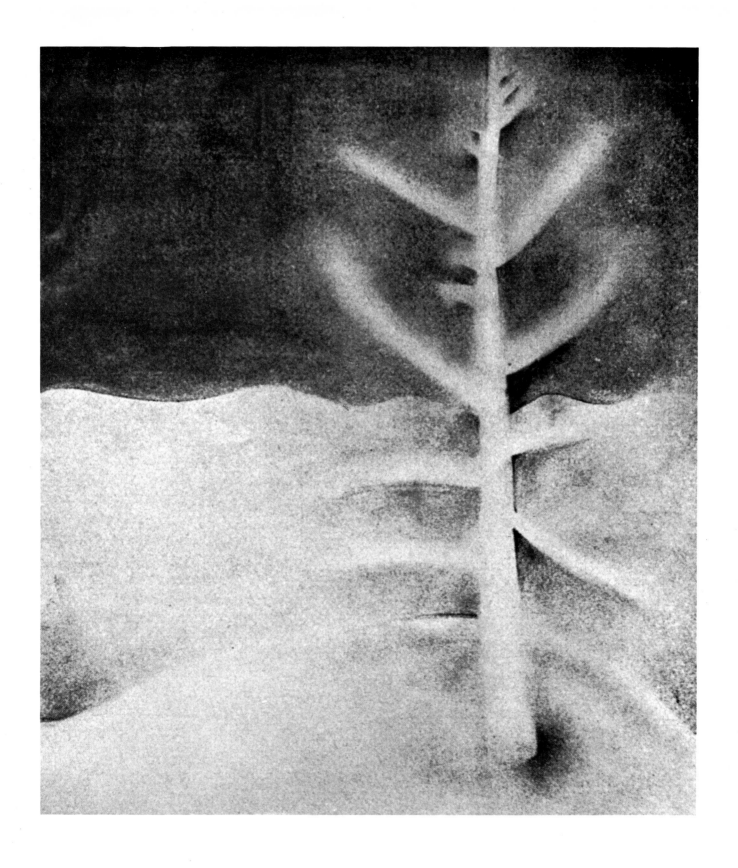

23 Tree in frost. This assignment shows the expressive potential of light-dark values. Berlin, 1929. P. Schmidt.

24 Nude study, composed as a design of light and shadow. Berlin, 1928. E. Bäumer.

25 Free composition on the theme "outing" was given as a monthly assignment after study of light-dark problems. The light and dark, large and small spots stand in a lively relationship and present the theme as cheerful play. Berlin, 1929. I. Hirschlaff.

26 Study of the placement of light-dark in the theme of a jumping dog. Equal tones bind; unequal tones repel. The white dog is attracted by white and repelled by black; it can jump. The black dog cannot jump if it is held from behind by black and repelled by the white area in front. Berlin, 1929. A. Rehse.

27 "Annunciation of St. Anne" by Giotto.

28 Analysis of Giotto's "Annunciation of St. Anne." In this painting Giotto has used light-dark in an elementary manner. Giotto's light-dark effect and compositional intent can be clearly recognized. Giotto has created the mystery of the Annunciation by placing the figures abstractly into the light-dark of the space. Vienna, 1918. M. Tery-Adler.

30 This analysis does not seek slavish imitation of the original painting; the spiritual content of the angel motif is to be revealed as an expressive quality of light-dark. Vienna, 1918. M. Cyrenius.

It was a cardinal principle of my teaching always to formulate assignments simply and clearly.

In the study of color, I eliminated all searching for form. The first assignment consisted of composing color spots side by side and overlapping each other. The students usually started by drawing the outlines of spots and coloring them afterwards. They paid attention to form and not to color. As early as 1917 I made the students use the chessboard division for most exercises in order to free the study of color effects from associations of form.

The student can discover the secrets of the color world only by painting. Learning to mix colors exactly after natural color spots or other samples furthers observation and color sense.

Working out the twelve-part color circle is the foundation of my color theory. The construction starts with the three basic colors: yellow, blue, red. Exact mental images are essential for these basic colors: Yellow must not tend towards yellowish green nor towards orange. Blue must not tend towards bluish green nor towards bluish red. Red must not tend towards reddish orange nor towards reddish blue. All three basic colors must be clearly represented, checked by the teacher, and painted into the three parts of an equilateral triangle. Then the three secondary colors, orange, violet and green, are to be produced by mixing the basic colors and entered according to the illustration. The six colors are placed in the respective sections of the twelve-part color circle. The remaining intermediate colors can then be found easily (Fig. 31).

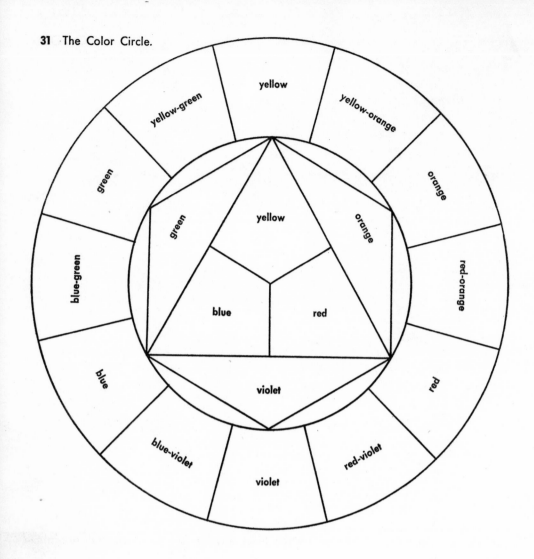

There are seven distinct contrast effects in the world of color:

1. **The contrast of hue:**
   It is produced by combining pure colors; white and black can heighten the vivid effect.

2. The light-dark contrast:
   This refers to the different degrees of lightness and tone values of colors. All colors can be lightened with white and darkened with black. First, tone scales of each color should be made which correspond to the light-dark scale (Fig. 11).

3. The cold-warm contrast:
   Its greatest contrast effect is reached with the colors orange-red and blue-green. All other colors appear cold or warm according to their juxtaposition with warmer or colder values.

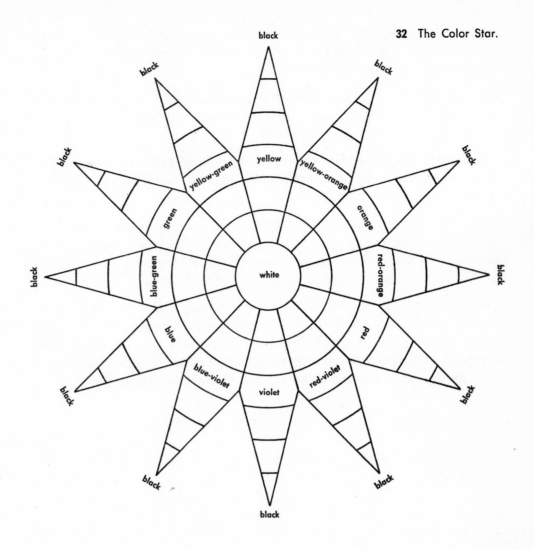

4. The complementary contrast:
   In my color circle the complementary colors stand opposite each other. Mixing complementary colors produces a neutral gray-black. Adjoining complementary colors intensify each other to greatest brilliance; mixed, they destroy each other.

5. The simultaneous contrast:
   Its effect is based on a corresponding law of complementaries. Each pure color physiologically demands its opposite color or complementary. If it is not present, the eye simultaneously produces the complementary color. A strong green makes an adjoining neutral gray appear reddish gray; a strong red gives a greenish gray effect to the same gray.

6. The contrast of saturation:
   It consists in the opposition of brilliant and dull colors. Dulling can be effected by adding black, white, gray or the complementary color.

7. The contrast of extension:
   It consists in opposing color areas of different sizes.

After studying and painting these contrasts, assignments should be given which bring the expressive qualities of color into view. Such themes are: Night, Baptism, Funeral, Fair, The Seasons.

The students learn that an appropriate coloration must be found for each theme. This leads to the realization that subjective taste does not always make an objectively correct color judgment.

General and comprehensive work with the world of color is necessary. The order of colors in the color sphere and general harmony are therefore essential.

The color star, the projection of the color sphere's surface in a plane, with the gradations of the twelve principal colors towards black and white, gives a good view of the total structure of color (Fig. 32). I developed this color star in 1921. It formed the basis of my color theory at the Bauhaus.

The world of color should be studied with brush and paints as well as demonstrated with colored examples. In my book, "The Art of Color," the various contrasts and possibilities are comprehensively presented and discussed with many color exercises and reproductions. This short treatment must be limited to the theory and method of my color teaching.

Exercises with materials and textures in the Basic Course at the Bauhaus proved especially stimulating.

As an introduction, long lists of different materials, like wood, glass, textiles, barks, furs, metals and stones, were written down. Then I had the students add the optical and tactile qualities of these materials. But it was not enough to know the words for these qualities, the characters of the materials had to be experienced and represented. Contrasts like smooth-rough, hard-soft, and light-heavy had to be not only seen but felt. I always attached great value to this sensuous grasping of the characteristic qualities of all things.

When I later directed a course in which architects, painters, and teachers were to be introduced to the problems of the Bauhaus Basic Course, I gave a still life as the first assignment. Two yellow lemons lay on a white plate, and there was a book with a green cover. The participants were almost offended by having to draw something so simple. The outlines were drawn with a few quick strokes, and everyone looked at me questioningly, no doubt expecting an introduction to geometric form problems. Without a word I took a lemon, cut it and gave everybody a piece to eat with the remark, "Have you represented the essence of the lemon in your drawing?" Sour-sweet laughter was the reply, and all began again to study the still life intensively.

At the Bauhaus I had long chromatic rows of real materials made for the tactile judging of different textures. The students had to feel these textures with their fingertips, their eyes closed. After a short time the sense of touch improved to an amazing degree. I then had the students make texture montages of contrasting materials. The effect of these fantastic creations was entirely novel at that time (Figs. 34, 36).

In solving these problems the students developed a real designing fever. They began to rummage through the drawers of thrifty grandmothers, their kitchens and cellars; they ransacked the workshops of craftsmen and the rubbish heaps of factories and building sites. A whole new world was discovered: lumber and wood shavings, steel wool, wires, strings, polished wood, and sheep's wool, feathers, glass, and tin foil, grids and weaves of all kinds, leather, furs, and shiny cans.

Manual abilities were discovered and new textures invented (Fig. 40). They started a mad tinkering, and their awakened instincts discovered the inexhaustible wealth of textures and their combinations. The students observed that wood could be fibrous, dry, rough, smooth, or furrowed; that iron could be hard, heavy, shiny, or dull. Finally they investigated how these textural qualities could be represented. These studies were of great value to the future architects, craftsmen, photographers, graphic artists, and industrial designers.

The various yarns, weaves, and technical processes provide a wide field of experimentation for textile designers (Figs. 61, 62). Developing the sense of touch is of fundamental importance for all workers with textiles. I therefore gave problems in textures and texture contrasts also to textile merchants, technicians, and managers.

To deepen and control experience, I had the students look at, touch, and draw materials such as wood, bark, and fur, until they were able to represent them by heart (Figs. 48, 49, 50). This kind of nature study, reproducing observation and experience from memory, is interpretive, not imitative. The results have direct vivid and convincing effects.

Through these exercises the student also learns to characterize appearances of the environment as textures, which he would not have recognized as such without them.

Repeated multiple units assume the expression of textures. A market, a crowd, a city, a railroad station lend themselves to a new kind of design (Figs. 55, 56, 59, 60).

When collages of photographed textures or textural effects from illustrations are combined with freely invented textures, the eye is educated for nonobjective vision. Only when he has reached this stage can the designer really compose textures.

33 Montage of various materials. Non-sculpturally used materials can have the effect of texture contrasts like transparent-opaque, horizontal-vertical, much-little, light-dark, straight-bent. Berlin, 1926.

34 To learn the characters of various textures, the students had to make montages of natural materials with contrast effects like smooth-rough, dull-shiny, transparent-opaque, vaulted-flat. Weimar, 1920.

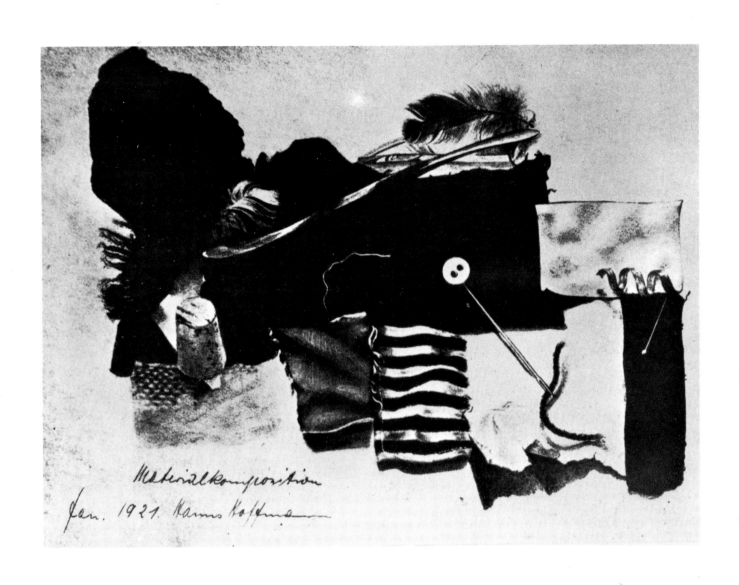

Materialkomposition
Jan. 1921. Hanns Hoffmann

35 Textures are clearly characterized as a material composition and balanced harmoniously. Weimar, 1921. Hanns Hoffmann. .

36   Relief composition of various textured materials. This kind of composing develops a feeling for textures and their optical and tactile intensities. Weimar, 1922. W. Diekmann.

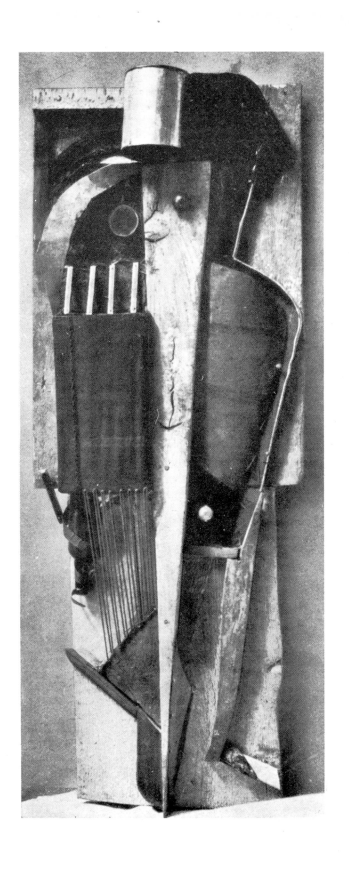

37 Three-dimensional study of diverse materials. The primary effect of the approximately 4 ft. high composition lies in the form contrasts: triangle, rectangle, circle, cylinder, point and line. The differentiation of the form effects through textures is only secondary. Weimar, 1922. W. Herzger.

38 Composition of wood, glass, and feathers. Transparent, shiny, hard, rigid glass is contrasted with soft, mobile feathers and opaque, firm wood. Weimar, 1920. M. Tery-Adler.

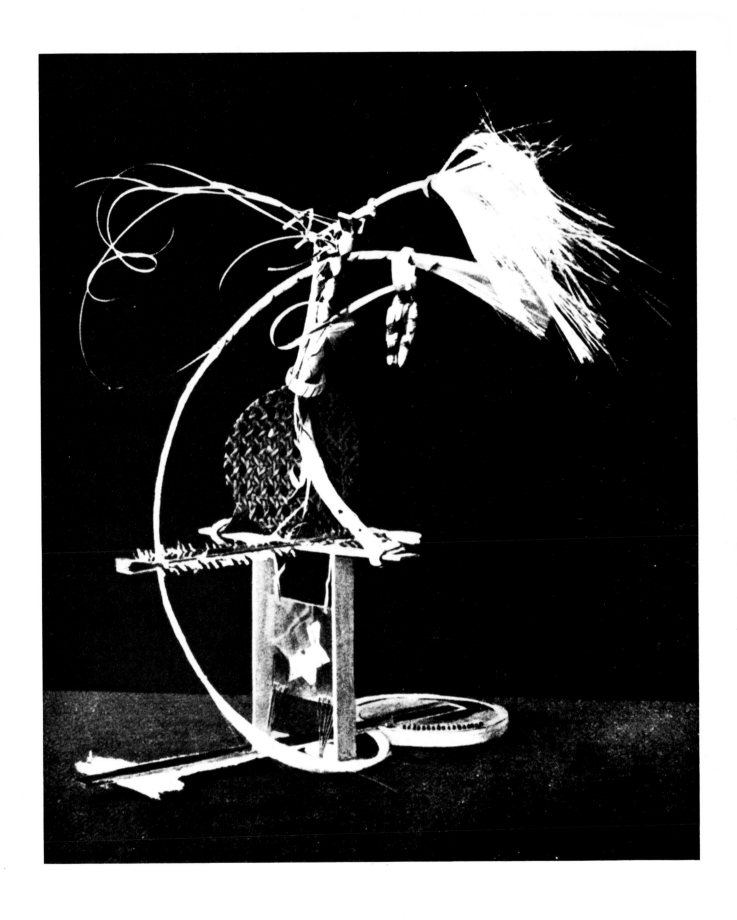

39 Spatial, three-dimensional montage with rhythmic and textured forms. The contrasting form effects are held together by differentiated rhythmic tensions. Weimar, 1921. M. Bronstein.

40 Texture developed on damp paper with India ink and pen. At that time the students searched eagerly for combs, brushes, sieves, oil and paste, to be able to invent new textures. Weimar, 1921. W. Menzel.

41 A future wood sculptor tests the possibilities of his material and tools. The apprentice had to carve textures into a board with different knives, without being encumbered by objective forms. Weimar, 1922. H. Busse.

42 The most diverse natural materials are composed in horizontal-vertical order. This assignment was given in a class for textile designers to develop fingertip feeling for the characters of various materials. Zurich, Textile Trade School, 1945.

43 Printed textures were sought in magazines, cut out and combined as a montage. Such exercises expand vision and enrich the student's own world of forms. Berlin, 1933. L. Müller.

44 Freely developed texture. Zurich, Textile School, 1960. W. Jaeger.

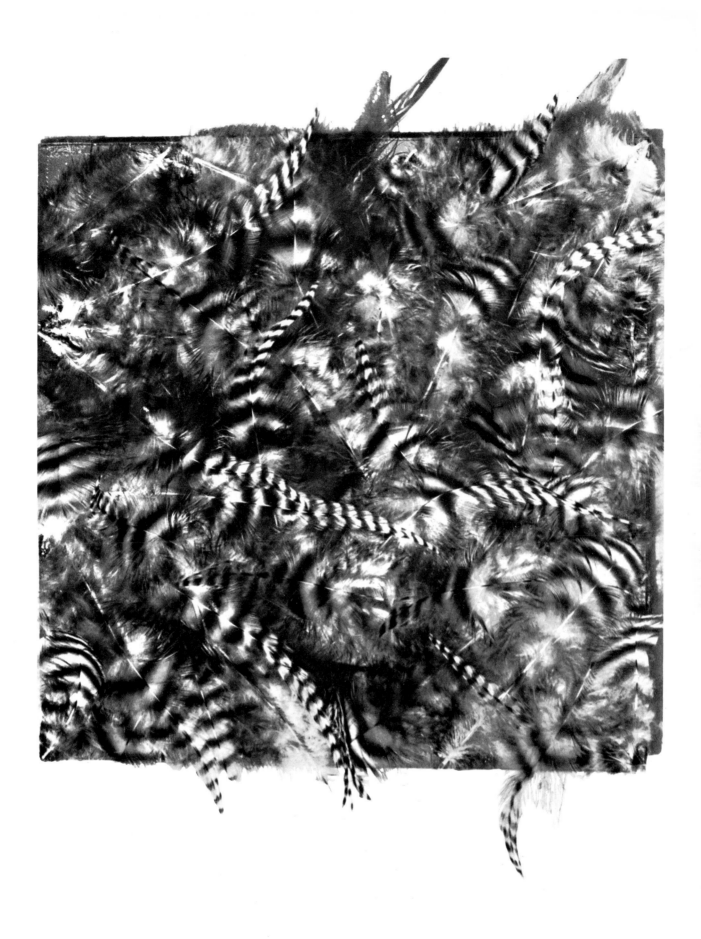

45 Montage of feathers. Textile students must develop a special feeling to be able to judge the touch of fabrics. All texture studies and montages afford a valuable opportunity to study nature beyond drawing. Zurich, Textile Trade School, 1960. A. Meier.

46 Texture drawings after nature composed in square areas. Berlin, 1929. Engeln-Hasbach.

47 A montage of natural textures interpreted through painting. Such studies are indispensible to test the student's ability to experience. Berlin, 1930.

48 A piece of wood, drawn from memory. Such assignments sharpen the senses, deepen the ability to observe, and increase proficiency in technical representation. Weimar, 1922. L. Leudesdorff-Engstfeld.

49 Birch bark, drawn from memory. Drawing from impulse produces forms of convincing, vivid power. Krefeld, 1934. R. Schalt.

62

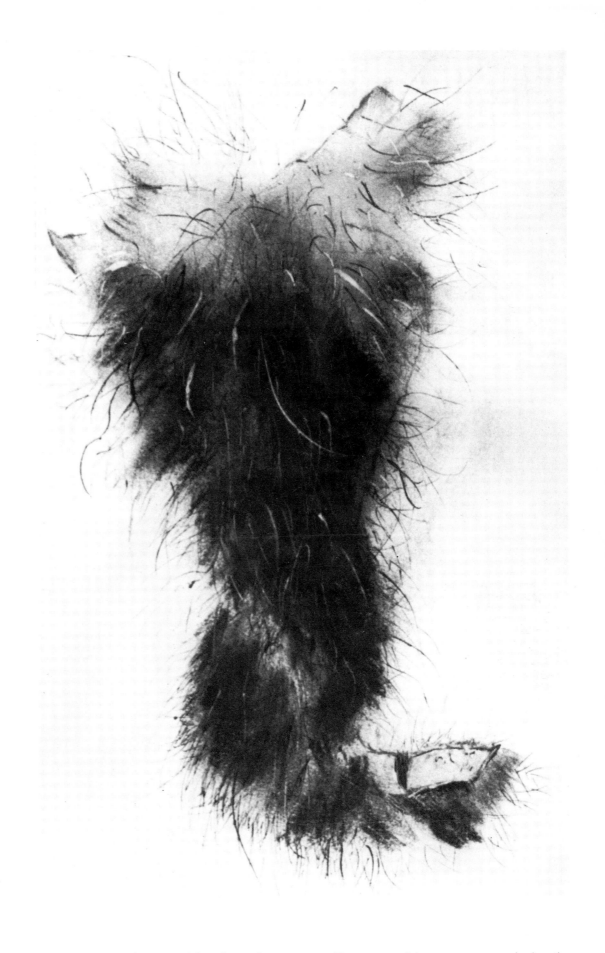

50 A piece of fur, drawn from memory. The texture of fur was represented after the experience of touching. Berlin, 1929. E. Elsner.

51 Corn cob and leaves, drawn from nature. The texture contrast between the shiny, three-dimensional kernels with the flat, dried, ribbed leaves and the hard, woody stalk is represented vividly. Krefeld, 1934. J. Hansen.

64

52 Nature study in light-dark and texture contrast. Various freely composed textures characterize the blossoms and leaves of the plant. Krefeld, 1934. H. Sieves.

53 The material studies stimulated the students to search for rare textures. The back of a cabbage leaf is rendered with black and colored pencils. Krefeld, 1934. R. Schalt.

54 India ink drawing of elder in bloom. The light blossoms in the sun and the dark blossoms in the shade, the transparent cluster and the dark leaves produce an image of differentiated texture and tones. Zurich, Textile Trade School, 1956. J. Bless.

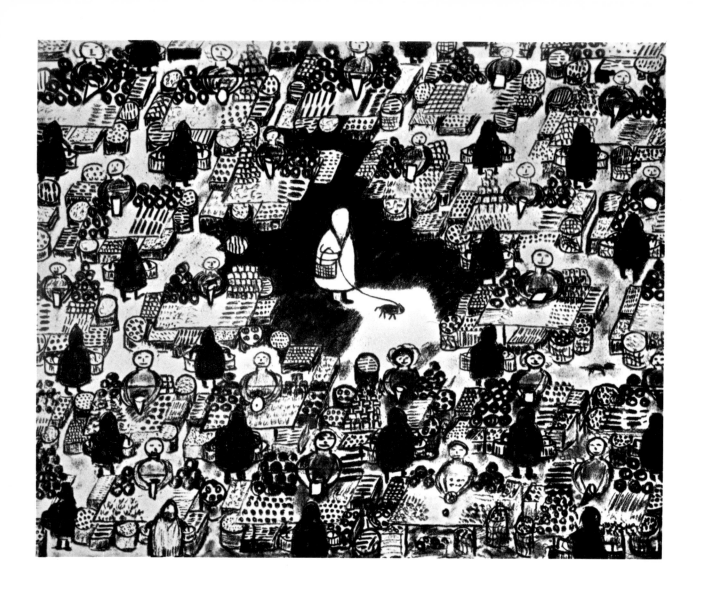

55 Viewed from an airplane, a market appears as a texture. Without an airplane, inner concentration is required to realize such an image. Such monthly themes were given to stimulate the students to seek new view-points and points of departure, to leave the model, to seek and represent new form relations. Berlin, 1931. H. Bleek.

56 This assignment, a crowd, shows the usefulness of texture studies. As in the preceding illustration, the student has not taken the photographic viewpoint. He has presented the theme in a unified form without attempting perspective. Through such exercises the student loses the tendency to imitate nature. He learns to interpret a given theme freely. Berlin, 1928. P. Schmidt.

57 This landscape was freely invented and composed with texture and form contrasts. Striving for clear expression demands geometrization and simplification. The non-perspective presentation allows a more expressive arrangement of proportions. Weimar, 1920. G. Stölzl.

58 The theme "village" demands a design in which a group of a few houses appears small among the surrounding fields. The fields, not the houses, dominate. Various landscape textures are suggested; this also tells something about the essence of village life. Berlin, 1931. A. Tsaussoglu.

59 Collage: The City. A confusing conglomeration of multiples, of verticals, horizontals and diagonals, of small rectangles, windows, bridges, passages and forms of all kinds gives the illusion of the endless tangle of a noisy big city. The multiple standpoints and view produce a synthetic picture. Weimar, 1921. P. Citroen.

These monthly assignments, double theme of village-city, were voluntarily done at home, and students only rarely failed to bring in homework. The class discussions of the solutions were among the most valuable hours because we touched on the subject of form expression. The students were able to compare their creative powers and to find a standard for their own performance.

60 The railroad station. All kinds of black ironwork and sooty glass were characteristic of large railroad stations in 1919. Idea and technique have captured the essence of the theme. The students' minds were free of preconceived theoretical notions; both compositions, city and railroad station, were created by P. Citroen within a short time. Weimar, 1919. P. Citroen.

61 Hand-knotted Smyrna rug. The effect of texture studies on this work is evident. The knotting technique permits the use of diverse materials. This rug was made before the actual weaving workshop was established at the Bauhaus. Weimar, 1921. G. Stölzl.

62 Woven fabric design. At the Textile Pattern School in Krefeld I had texture studies executed on small handweaving frames. The fabric sketches were made of various materials and yarns in appropriate weaves without preliminary designs. The idea of the fabric was then worked out and studied up to the stage of industrial production. Krefeld, 1936.

63 Striped fabric, woven of transparent cellophane threads and thick artificial silk; demonstrates the contrast transparent-opaque. Krefeld, 1935. J. Hansen.

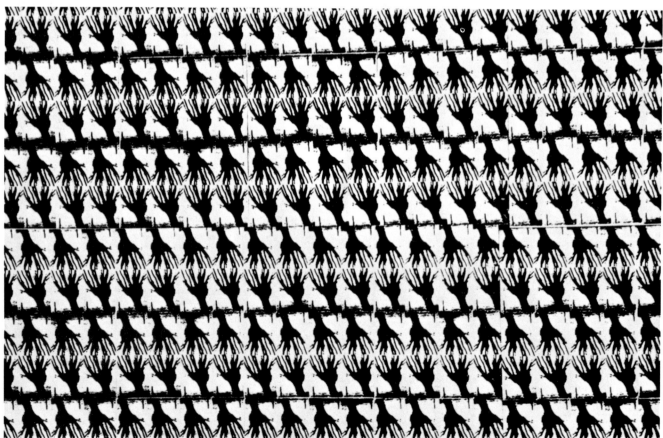

64 – 66 Photomontages. All objects of the environment, even the most insignificant, become significant for form-sensitive people at a certain time in a certain relationship of light-dark or texture contrasts. Plants, landscapes, bridges, streets, tar barrels, machine parts, window shutters provide new stimuli. Photography is an important medium for an expanded view of nature. It also permits insights into the microworld and opens an inexhaustible field of new forms. Krefeld, 1936.

67 At the Krefeld Pattern Design School new artistic and technical ways of fabric printing were sought. Varnish, gold and fluorescent prints were created. It was not the task of the fabric printing workshop to imitate industrial products on a small scale or to vary their patterns, but to awaken the students' interest for creative work. How can an industrial designer daily invent something new if his creative abilities and powers have not been awakened? The illustration shows the idea of a design for a silk fabric. The pattern was developed from a fingerprint; a photomontage of this print led to a surprising new texture. The design was executed as a mat print on glossy white silk. Krefeld, 1935. O. Stocken.

68 Freely developed texture as print design. Zurich, Textile Trade School, 1959. S. Rey.

The assignments in abstract form composition serve to improve thinking and, at the same time, to work out new means of design. These exercises in form were not formalistic style exercises as they are commonly understood today. The three basic forms, the square, the triangle, and the circle, are characterized by the four different spatial directions. The character of the square is horizontal and vertical; the character of the triangle is diagonal; the character of the circle is circular.

I first tried to convey these three forms as an experience. I made the students stand and trace a circle with the arm until the whole body was in a relaxed, swinging motion. This exercise was carried out with the left and the right arm, first singly and then together, in the same and in the opposite directions. Thus the circle was experienced as an evenly curved line in continuous motion. Then followed concentration on the circle as form; it had to be felt without moving the body. Only then followed drawing the circle on paper.

Experiencing the square requires an angular, tense form of movement because the right angle always recurs.

In the triangle the whole diversity of angles appears.

The variations and contrasts of forms were worked out in series of exercises (Figs. 69, 81, 82, 86). Compositions of square, triangular, and circular character were made to awaken an understanding for unity of form (Figs. 72, 74, 84). Further exercises are derived from combinations of two or three forms (Figs. 89, 90, 99, 100).
Then followed form divisions of square, triangular, and circular character. The decorative fabric design of unified square character (Fig. 73) is based on the principle of progression. The problems of proportion were investigated in lines, planes, and volumes.

Lines can be developed whose sections are determined through proportionate numbers. The sequence of these numbers can be varied. Proportions like $1 : 2 : 4 : 8 : 16 : 32$ or $1 : 3 : 9 : 81$ can be represented. The Golden Section and the proportions of the harmonic triangle must be studied. These proportions have to be constructed and contrasted as lines, planes, and volumes.

The student learns that contrasts of proportions can achieve effects which no longer correspond to the reality of numbers. It is well known that a long form can be made to appear much longer by contrasting it with a short form. These simultaneous changes of proportions can only be judged by feeling; they give to proportions an unreal vividness which is sought and used by the artist.

Exercises in variation and combination also serve to promote thinking. Four matches can become a vivid experience for the student. These little sticks with heads provide an infinite number of new figures — through horizontal, vertical or diagonal shifts; through rotations, reflections, and sliding reflections; reversals, overlappings, changes of proportion, tone and color changes, and through combinations of these variations. The creative imagination should have many possibilities at its command to produce a work of art. Thinking in terms of variations and combinations must be developed through exercises, so that the simplest and clearest form is found. Figs. 97, 98, 99 show variations and combinations of a line motif which is built of circular, square, and triangular elements.

The study of three-dimensional forms and their representation is of great importance. I first had the students model spheres, cubes, pyramids, cones, and cylinders in clay, so that they could feel these forms three-dimensionally. Then compositions based on a single form were modeled. Figs. 111 and 112 show such compositions of cubic characters; these are not architectural designs. Finally, I had the students execute compositions with two or three form characters.

Only after these modeling exercises were the three-dimensional forms rendered graphically with light and shadow in imitative fashion (Fig. 118). As a second exercise, the representation of three- dimensional forms had to be worked out as a flat pattern, the naturalistic three-dimensional effect is dematerialized, producing a pictorial plane.

If we want to give the illusion of spatial depth without destroying the picture plane, careful use of diagonals, overlappings, tones, and colors is required. Figs. 120, 121, 123 and the analyses in Figs. 122 and 124 show treatments of such problems of pictorial space.

The effect of a composition is largely determined by the right distribution of accents. This applies not only to art but also to dance, music, and poetry.

The points of accent give tension to a picture and direct the viewer's eye. His glance glides from accent to accent; he thus feels intervals and experiences simultaneous connecting lines. These lines provide paths of vision, and they in turn enclose forms which have to be carefully studied in their size relations (Fig. 102). Definite points of accent belong to each form. All points of accent which lie on the axes or diagonals of a form are good points. When one point of accent dominates, the viewer's eye will rest on it longer than on accompanying, weaker points; the glance will always return to the major accent. A major accent leads the viewer into quiet depth of vision, while several points of equal accent call for gliding vision and thus the experience of motion. It is also possible to make accent analyses and line analyses from nature (Fig. 104). I can only hint at the problems of pictorial construction here. The geometric-constructive organization of the picture plane connects points of accent and reinforces the structure.

Pictorial constructions should be developed from the first sketches. They serve to find the ultimate format and help to bring the incidentals of the first sketch into the order of the picture plane.

If a plane is to be divided formally, there is an infinite number of possibilities. The chess board, the perfect plane composition, divides the plane by a single repeated form. The black and the white squares are reductions of the form of the whole board. Other forms which can fill a plane completely are the rectangle, the rhombus, the triangle, and the equilateral hexagon. Starting from these basic divisions, a large number of additional forms can be found. These positive-negative congruent forms are the most severe forms of plane divisions (Figs. 125 - 133, 134, 135). Their study strengthens and deepens logical form thinking.

69 Exercise in the form character of the square. The square and its derivations in horizontal-vertical character are composed in contrasting series of proportions. Weimar, 1920. M. Pfeiffer-Watenphul.

IM ZIMMER WAR. WO SIND WOHL SIE WOHL, FRAGTE ER
SICH? DA DIE SONNE HIER IN DEN TROPEN SEHR HEISS IST,
UND ES ZUDEM SEHR FEUCHT WAR, WUNDERTE ER SICH,
DIE GANZE GESELLSCHAFT NICHT IM KÜHLEN HAUSE
ZU FINDEN. BEI DIESER DRÜCKENDEN HITZE GING ER

UMS HÄUSL HERUM UND SAH SIE ALLE IM SCHATTEN
EINER PALME UM EINEN TÜMPEL HERUMSITZEN. SIE
SCHIENEN SEHR FRÖHLICH, UND BEIM NÄHERTRETEN
SAH ER, DASS MANDA EINEN KLEINEN JUNGEN
AFFEN IN DEN HÄNDEN HIELT.

70 Square character in writing and illustration. I also made the students write such exercise sheets in triangular and circular characters to awaken a feeling for the unity of a form. Zurich, Art and Crafts School, 1950.

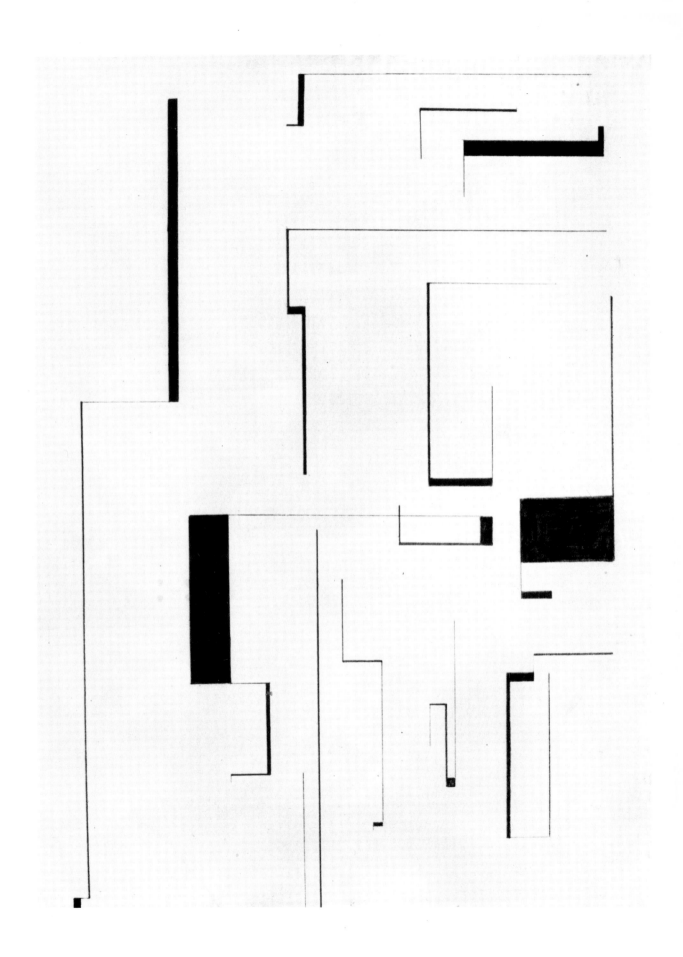

71 Study sheet of various line exercises of square character. The contrasts horizontal-vertical, long-short and broad-narrow are used. Berlin, 1928. M. Debus.

72 Study sheet with area compositions of square character with the contrasts light-dark, broad-narrow. Berlin, 1928.

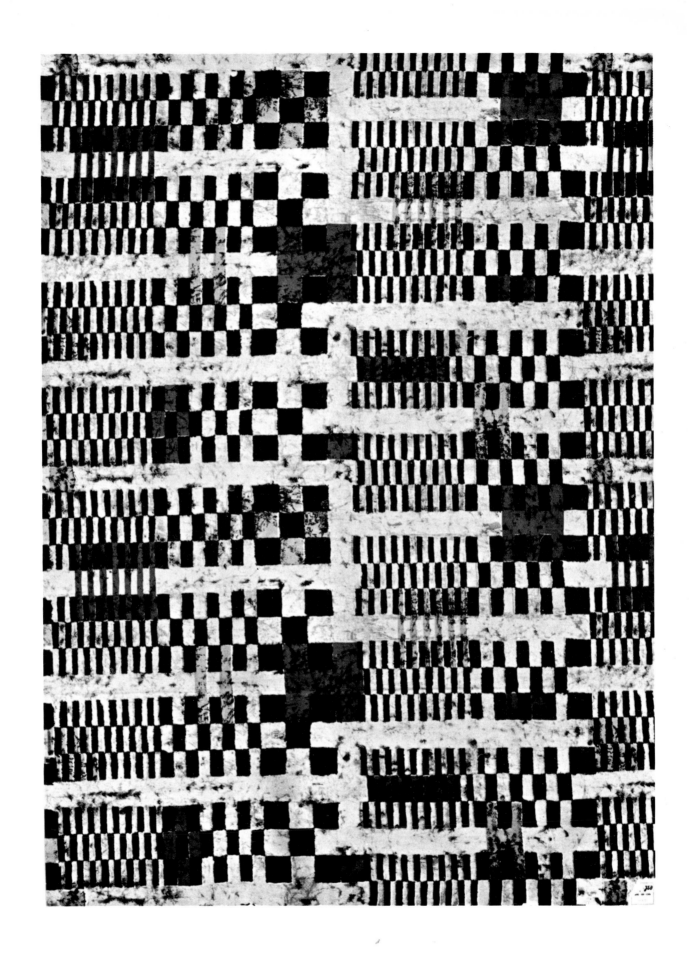

73 Decorative fabric, printed with progressively developed form elements of the square. Zurich, Textile Trade School, 1957. I. Oechslin.

74 Form composition developed from square character. Relief effect through the application of light-dark. Weimar, 1921. G. Teltscher.

75 Wooden relief of a door with nickel-plated handle developed from square and cubic characters. Working with a team of several students, I wanted to create a room of unified form elements. A man of a definite height was taken as module. The metal work was made in Weimar, 1921. N. Slutzky.

76—77 Division of a square by horizontals and verticals.

78 Division of a square by diagonals.

79 Division of a square by horizontals, verticals, and diagonals. Zurich, Arts and Crafts School.

80 The wall hanging in gobelin technique is a composition of square character with contrasts of color and proportion. The triangle was added as a form contrast. This work was given to me by the students at Christmas, 1920; it is now in the Bauhaus Archive at Darmstadt. Weimar, 1920. Design: M. Pfeiffer-Watenphul; Jointly executed by several students.

81 – 82 Two exercise sheets in the form character of the triangle. Weimar, 1919. F. Singer.

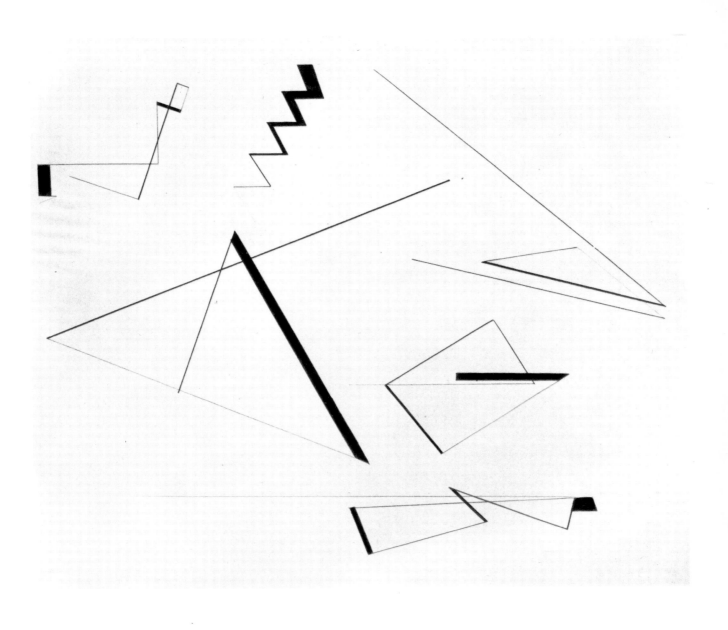

83 Study sheet with line composition in triangle character. It applies the contrasts long-short, broad-narrow, and variations of the angles. Berlin, 1928. M. Debus.

84 Division of a square in triangle character. Zurich, Textile Trade School, 1960. D. Kürner.

85 The wooden relief on a door of the Sommerfeld log house shows form contrasts of triangle and square characters with different textures. Weimar, 1922. Design and execution I. Schmidt.

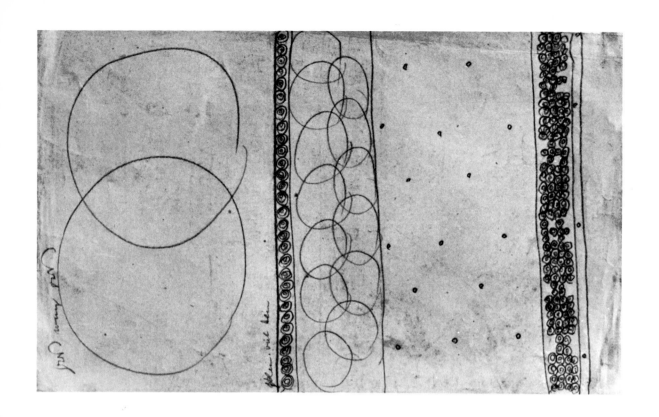

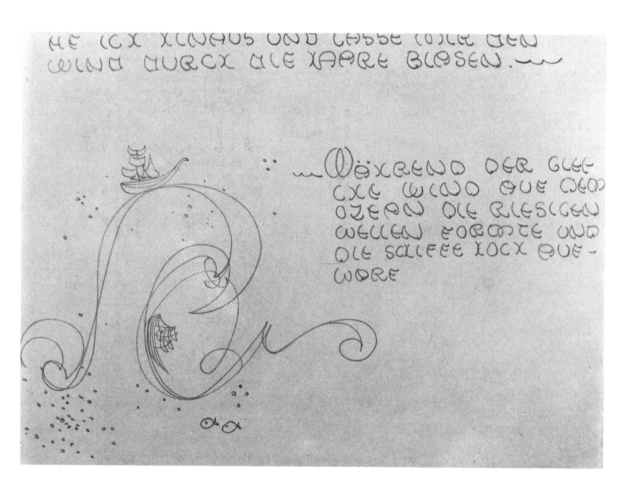

86 Exercise sheet in circular character. Weimar, 1919. F. Singer.

87 Circular character in writing and decorative form. Zurich, Arts and Crafts School.

88 Division of a circle in circular forms with different tone values. Zurich, Arts and Crafts School.

89 When two or three forms are used in one composition, they can be of equal value, or one form can be stressed while the others have only subordinate functions. Good feeling for form is necessary to arrange the various forces in a balanced whole. Weimar, 1919. F. Dicker.

90 Composition in light-dark and large-small contrast with the three form characters. Weimar, 1920. K. Auböck.

91 To make the relativity of proportion effects vividly clear to 8 – 10 year-old children, I gave the following assignment: "Lay your hand on the sheet and draw the outline of the hand with a pencil. Next to this hand draw in their natural size an apple – a plum – two cherries – two berries – and – on the hand a gnat."
The children found the correct proportions without trouble because they had already experienced them.
"Now draw me an elephant next to it!"
The children all cried it couldn't be done, the sheet was much too small.
I asked, "Is it impossible to draw elephants?" The children thought they had to take a new sheet.
They took the new sheet, and I continued to dictate: "Draw an old, big elephant – a young elephant next to it – the keeper – he stretches his hand out to the elephant – in the hand lies an apple – on it sits a gnat."
"Can't do it," cried the children again.
"Draw an elephant again and try to draw it so it looks very big – draw a little keeper next to it! Can you see that the elephant looks bigger with the little keeper?" Berlin, 1928.

98

92 The proportion contrasts large-small and broad-narrow are represented in light-dark contrast. Berlin, 1932. E. Kayser.

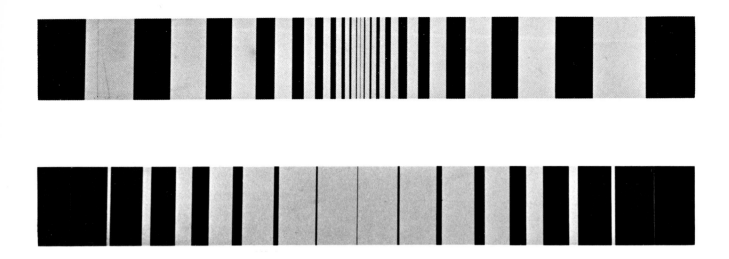

93–94 Scales of proportion from broad to narrow in parallel and opposed directions.

95 Lines in vertical and diagonal character composed as broad-narrow proportion contrasts. Berlin, 1928. M. Debus.

96 Study of proportion drawn from nature. Berlin, 1928. E. Bäumer.

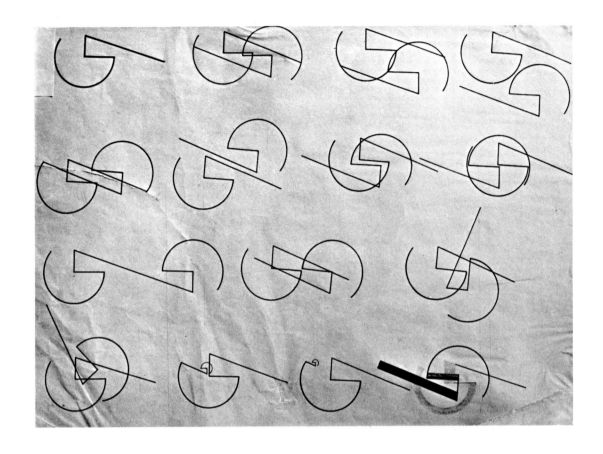

97–98 Combinations and variations of a line motif which is constructed of circular, square, and triangular elements. Two such lines are combined in reversal, in narrow and wide placement, in opposed motion, and in intersection. The large-small and light-dark contrasts are added as variation. Berlin, 1932. F. Windscheif.

99 The motif of Fig. 95 as a free composition. Berlin, 1932. F. Windscheif.

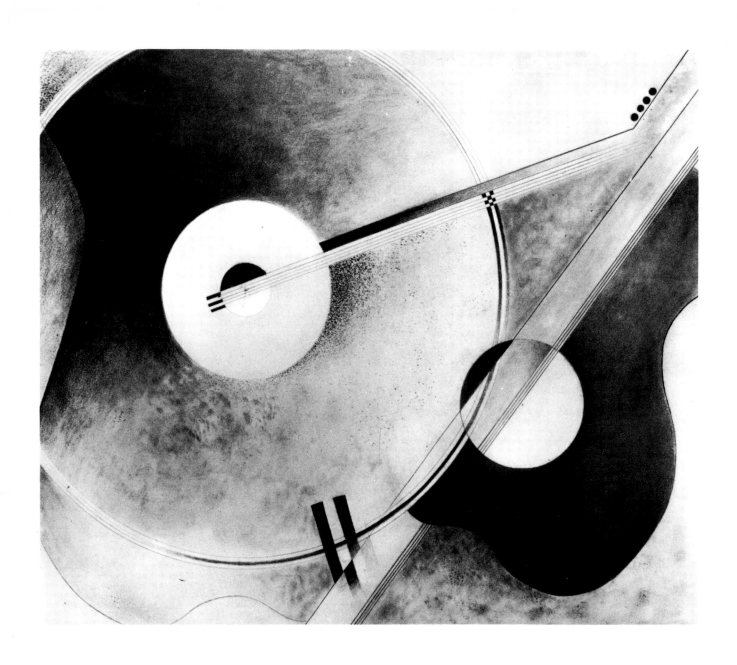

100 Composition in circular and triangular character. Berlin, 1928. A. Rehse.

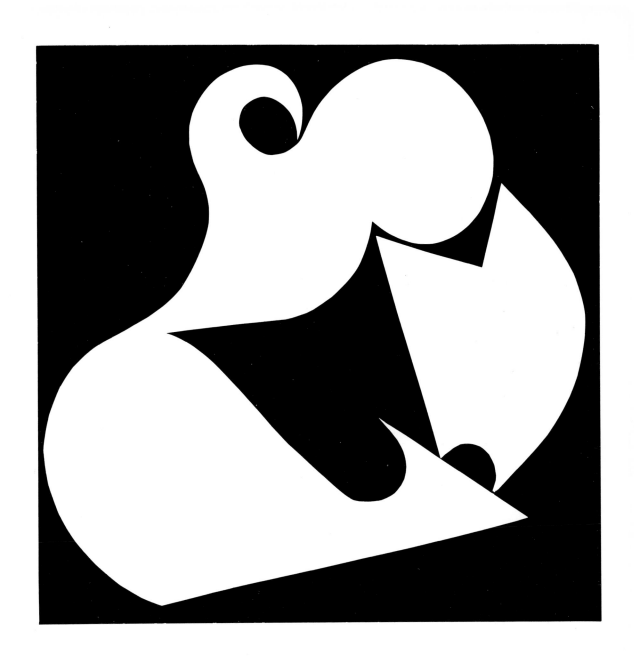

101 Free form figure. Berlin, 1928. P. Schmidt.

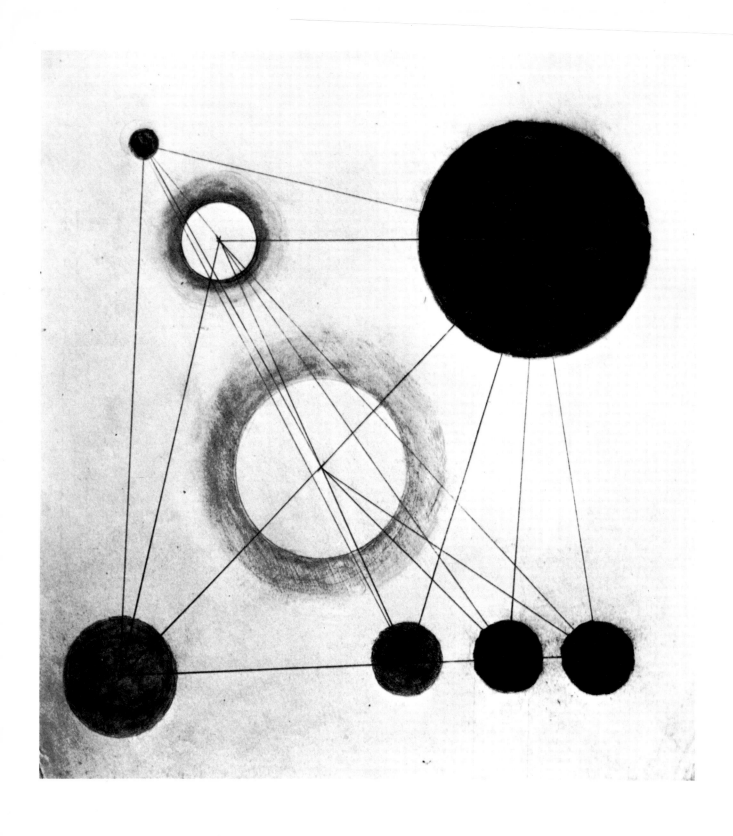

102 The placement and relation of accent points in a composition are to be carefully chosen. The connecting lines represent the possible paths of vision. Berlin, 1928. H. Stauch.

103 Scattered accent points are used in the representation of a meeting. Berlin, 1928. R. Rothe.

104 Study after a still life, constructively designed with lines and accent points. Berlin, 1928. R. Rothe.

105 The Class. A good arrangement of the heads in the room had to be found. Berlin, 1929. H. Müller.

106 Line analysis from nature. Berlin, 1929. E. Bäumer.

107 Abstracted forms of vessels freely composed into formal harmony. Such exercises lead to non-objective seeing of form. Berlin, 1928. E. Bäumer.

108–109 Simultaneous representation of a vase. Plan, elevation, three-dimensional and perspective form are represented in two different compositions. Berlin, 1933.

110 Composition of transparent, opaque, shiny, dull, textured and colored planes and volumes. Berlin, 1932. Molenaar

111 To make the students experience the elementary geometric forms three-dimensionally,
I had volumes like sphere, cylinder, cone, and cube modelled in clay. Weimar, 1921.
I. Mögelin.

114

112 This is not an architectural model but a study in cubic character. Some planes were painted to study how the colors can diminish or increase the three-dimensional effect. The wires suggest glass walls. Weimar, 1921. G. Schunke.

113 The wooden chest was executed as a workshop assignment after the study of form characters and textures in the Basic Course. Weimar, 1921. L. Gräf.

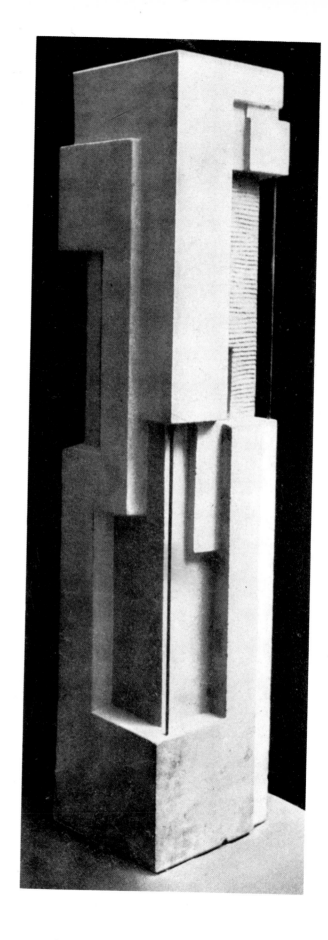

114 Architectural sculpture of cubic character, executed in sandstone. The relief corresponds to the work in Fig. 75 and Fig. 113. Weimar, 1921. K. Schwerdtfeger.

115 Hammered copper can. The spherical shape, its texturing by segments and the relation between the diameter of the sphere and the segments produce formal unity. The three-dimensional sphere is contrasted with the linear dotted texture. Weimar, 1920. N. Slutzky.

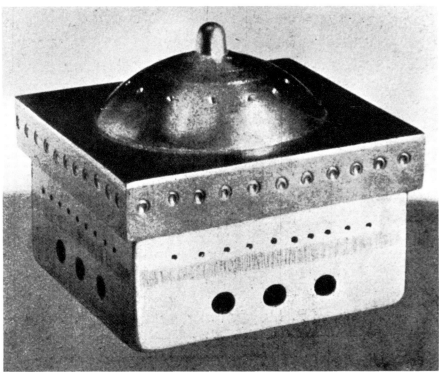

116 Brass can. The transition from the cylindrical basic form to the spherical lid is formed by a flat ring which functions as the handle of the lid. The linear ornament repeats the ring-shaped element. Weimar, 1920. K. Auböck.

117 Brass and copper can. The basic form of cubic character is contrasted with the spherical character of the lid. The ornament consists of larger and smaller circular ornaments. The problem here was to combine various form characters. Weimar, 1921. Lipovec.

118 The elementary volumes, cube, cone, sphere, and cylinder, are represented realistically, graphically, three-dimensionally. Berlin, 1928. F. Brill.

119 The elementary solids of Fig. 118 are represented as pictorial elements in a three-dimensional interpretation. The light-dark is arranged so that, in spite of the three-dimensional effect, no holes result in the picture plane. Berlin, 1928. F. Brill.

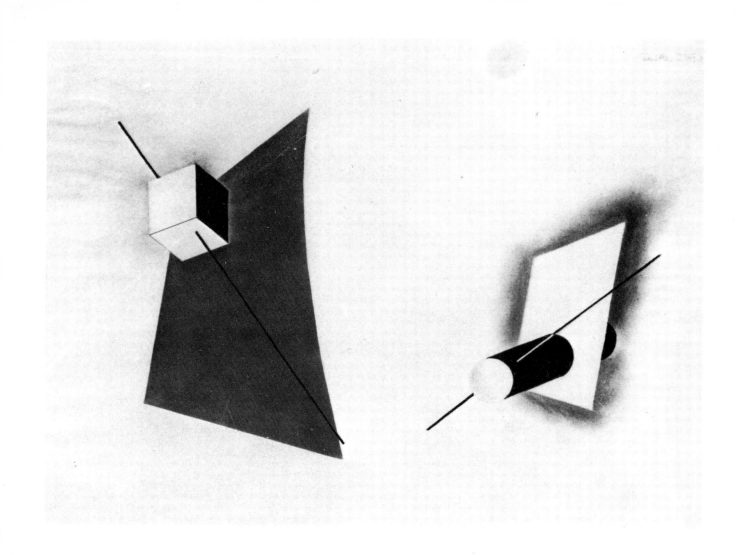

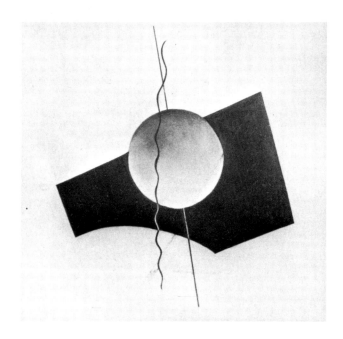

120–121 The assignment was to represent solid, plane and line as a flat picture. Berlin, 1929. G. Itting.

122 This analysis of the angel from the painting of the Annunciation by Petrus Christus was done after the pictorial space studies in Figs. 118 – 121. Berlin, 1929. U. Klemm.

123 Three-dimensional forms represented pictorially as light-dark. Berlin, 1932. L. Müller.

124 Analysis of a detail from "The Adoration of the Kings" by the Master of the Virgo inter Virgines is a study of this artist's pictorial use of spatial-three-dimensional and perspective elements. Berlin, 1932.

125—133 The chess board is the perfect plane division. The squares are a reduction of the total form. Other forms which divide a plane without leftovers are the triangle, the rhombus, and the hexagon. These basic forms can be varied by adding and simultaneously removing parts. I call these equal variation forms "positive-negative forms." They were already known in antiquity as wall and floor ornaments but offer a wide field of new forms. Here, several one- and two-color developments are reproduced. Krefeld, 1935. N. Diamantidi.

134 Printed fabric with positive-negative pattern. Krefeld, 1936. A. Diepgen.

135 Woven silk fabric with congruent plane forms. Krefeld, 1936.

136 Analysis of Memling's portrait of Willem Moreel; its purpose was to study the geometric-constructive organization of the picture plane. The guide lines, found by the student,
connect points of accent and reinforce the structure. Berlin, 1932. F. Windscheif.

Repetition or unison of points, lines, planes, spots, volumes, proportions, textures, and color produces rhythmic themes.

A rhythm can repeat itself in a characteristic regular beat, in up and down, strong and weak, long and short. But it can also be irregular, continuous, in free flowing movement.

There is great power in everything rhythmical. The rhythm of ebb and high tide changes the shorelines of the continents; the rhythmic dances of African tribes, lasting for days and nights, drive people to ecstasies.

Our young people experience rhythm in jazz and dance. This reasoning determined my way of introducing the students to monoform rhythmic design. First I had the students walk in march rhythm, beating time with their hands. The rigidity of this simplest rhythm was to take hold of the whole body. Then I counted off a triple rhythm, so that the stress fell first on the right foot, then on the left. Various changes followed, and sometimes two students would dance to the syncopated rhythm of a record.

Then these rhythms were drawn; the march rhythm was represented by stressed and unstressed strokes, the triple rhythm by circular elements. Varying intonation determined the motion. When a march or waltz rhythm was stopped after a few beats and continued in irregular intervals, the interruption of the rhythmic movement was felt almost painfully by everyone. To let the students experience the circular rhythm I had them stand and swing clubs or bottles in circles and figure eights. It was important to keep the mind concentrated on the rhythm of the movements.

All exercises had to be repeated graphically. The experience of flowing movement is very impressive when forms are related in continous harmony. I dictated a sentence to show that rhythmic sensation is not mere schematic repetition but can be a flowing movement. I then made the students write the sentence twice as fast, then three times as fast, finally as fast as possible. They were amazed to find that this produced the strangest letter forms, which were beyond deliberate control and showed a highly rhythmical correlation.

When the form of a simple object is added to the rapid writing, the individual rhythm of the handwriting is continued in this form; the form seems to belong to the handwriting (Fig. 140). This observation brings a deeper understanding of rhythmic design.

Rhythm can thus be explained and comprehended up to a certain point, but its innermost essence is inexplicable. The rhythmically handwritten forms have their own wind and breath which make them a living family of forms. Here is where the essence of true automatism appears. When the same letters are written without this breath, the letter forms stand there unrhythmically cold, unrelated, and unyielding.

Years ago, I visited a sculptor in his studio. He was working on two above-life-size female figures for a tomb. The first figure was satisfactory, but he had been working on the second figure for weeks without success. He had created the first figure and its rhythmic draperies with enthusiasm, and it was convincing. He did not succeed with the second figure because he began the work tired and without concentration; he tried to achieve through will and reason what can only succeed through intuition and free rhythmic feeling.

Both geometric abstract forms and natural forms were studied until the students were able to represent them in an uninterrupted motion. Figs. 139 and 141 show a brush and a charcoal drawing which were produced in this way. Even wholly different lines assume a rhythmic expression when they are written in one motion (Fig. 142).

Variation and combination exercises with the four match sticks are executed rhythmically in Fig. 145. It is essential to find the right sequence in the writing of the individual forms because the motion should be without interruption. One form must develop out of another with intermediary form elements.

Fig. 147 represents a progressive rotation of rhythmic movements and counter-movements. Besides rhythmic exercises in line, studies of rhythmic spots must be made. Here, too, studies after old masters can promote understanding for rhythmic design (Figs. 151, 152, 153).

137 Students write rhythmic forms simultaneously with both hands.
It is good to train the left and the right hand equally. The hands may draw or write in parallel or opposite directions. Such mirror writing succeeds only when the mental image of the letter forms is clear enough to be translated into the corresponding hand motions.

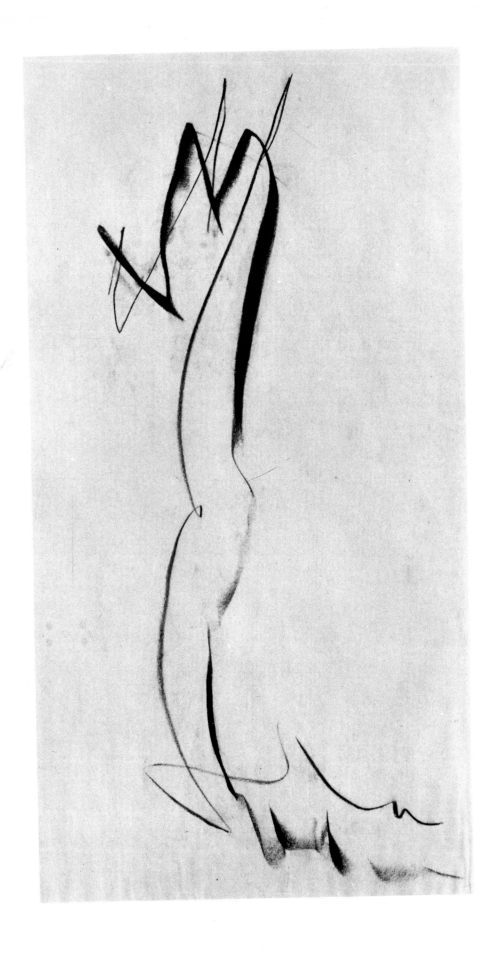

138 Ambidextrously drawn parallel rhythmic lines.

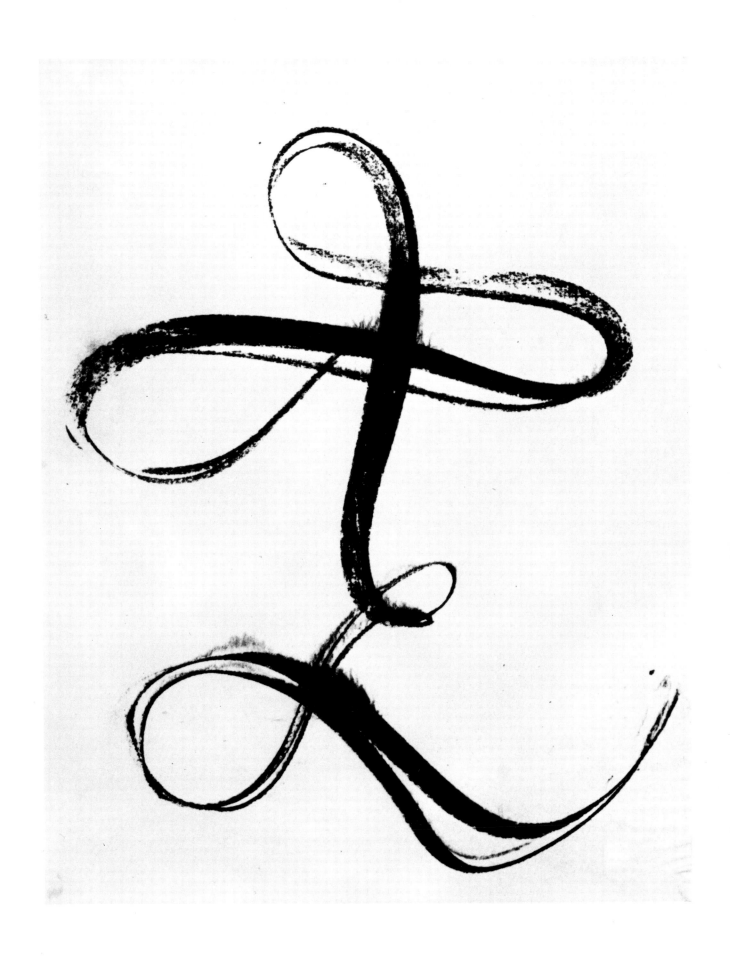

139 This swinging form was executed with two pieces of charcoal in one hand.

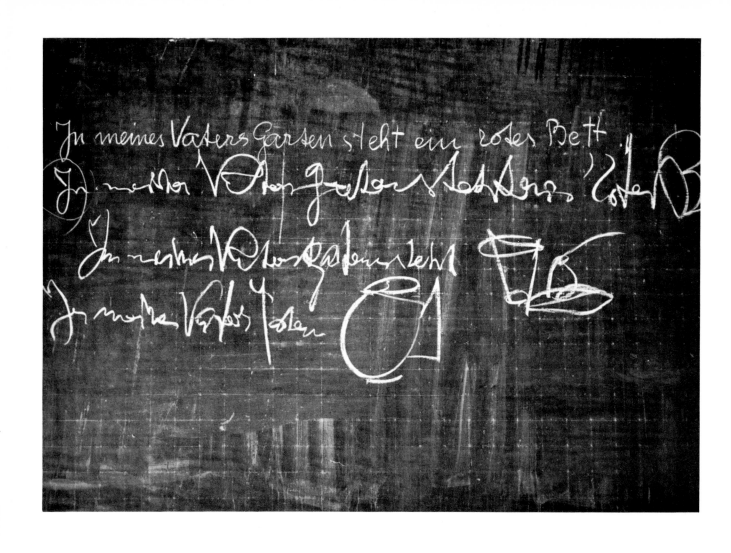

140 Blackboard drawing shows the development of rhythmic form relations in hand-writing. The first line is written normally and without special rhythmic expression. In lines 2, 3 and 4 the speed of writing was increased, and glass, plate, and pear were added in the same rhythm. The unconscious produced a rhythmic relation between the written and drawn forms.

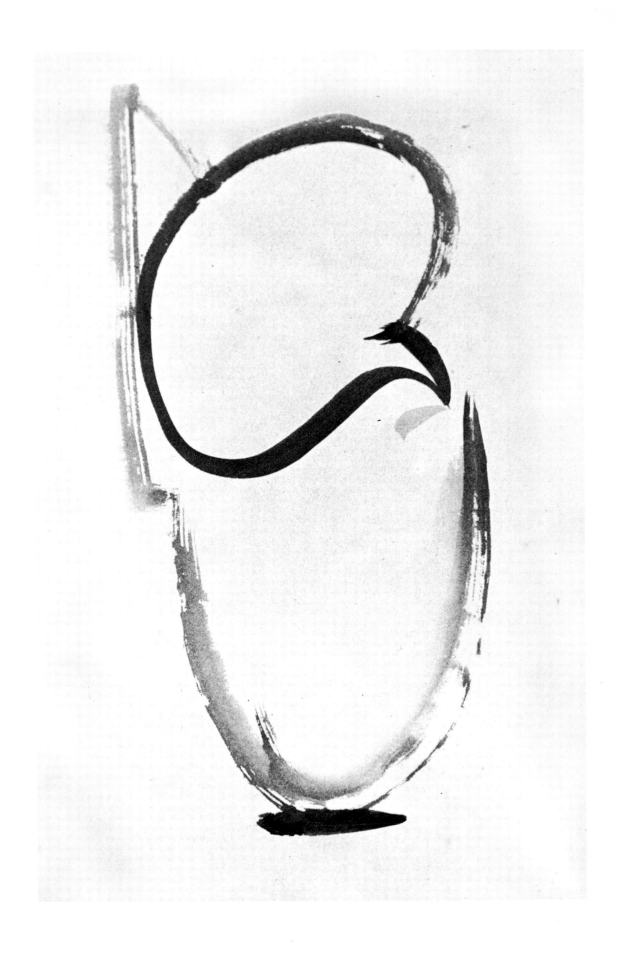

141 This pitcher was drawn with a brush in uninterrupted motion after the mental image of a pitcher had become clear.

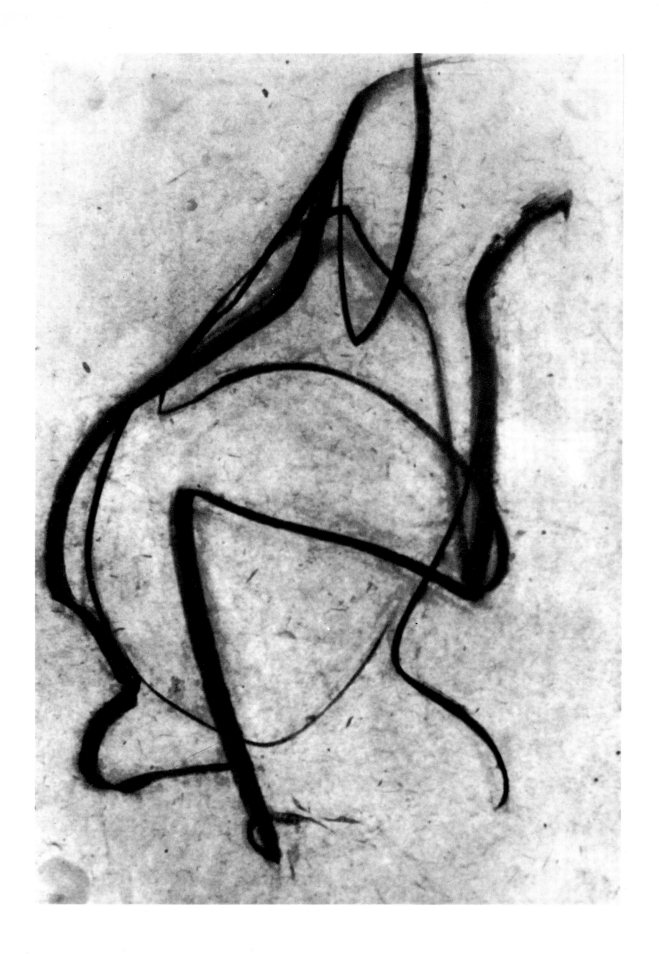

142 This form was found in intuitive and free linear rhythm without model or reference to a theme. Weimar, 1919. F. Dicker.

143 This broadly drawn form shows a rhythmic motion which is entirely different from the preceding illustration 142. Weimar, 1920. W. Graeff.

144 Rhythmic form of diagonals and acute angles with points of accent. Weimar, 1920.
W. Graeff.

145 Four matches, consisting of point and stroke, are the theme of this rhythmic exercise, in which each group of forms is written without interruption. The transitions from one form to the next must be found without losing the rhythm. Zurich, Textile Trade School, 1959. M. Frey.

146 The flowing wave motion, the arrested wave and the rigid meander are strong, rhythmically expressive contrasts. Weimar, 1920.

147 Motion, counter-motion, and rotation of rhythmic lines. Berlin, 1929.

148 If we want to draw a thistle, we must have experienced the stabbing points and opposing directions of the defending plant. The feeling for the aggressive thistle character should remain alive during the drawing to produce meaningful and expressive forms by violent, pointed, and stabbing motions. Weimar, 1920. G. Stölzl.

142

149 Mounted colored and structured forms in circular rhythm. Weimar, 1921. M. Pfeiffer-Watenphul.

150 This form has been realized by a powerful impulse. The dynamic basis of everything rhythmical is visibly expressed. Vienna, 1918. M. Tery-Adler.

151 The figure is drawn after a picture by Lucas Cranach, analyzing its rhythmic motion and omitting all details. Weimar, 1919. A. Wotiz.

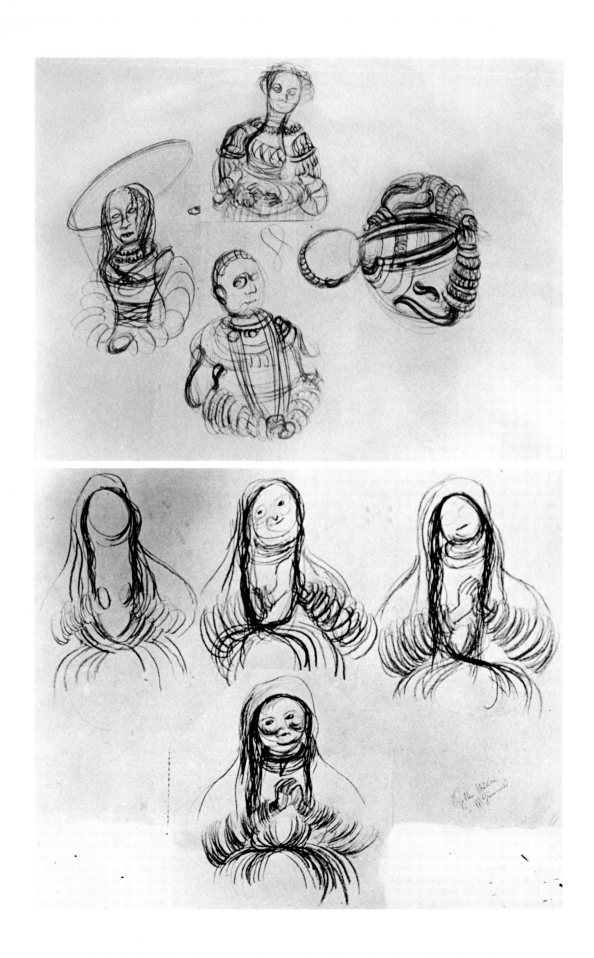

152–153 Analytical studies of rhythmic elements after figures by Lucas Cranach and Mathias Grünewald. Berlin, 1929.

146

Freeing and deepening the expressive ability of students is the teacher's most difficult task.

To execute the following exercises it is necessary to choose a very flexible, expressive medium which reacts immediately to the slightest motion of the hand, such as India ink brush or soft charcoal. Generally, students are careless with their painting tools. Brushes are used to color areas but they are not cared for like valuable expressive instruments.

If a genuine feeling is to be expressed in a line or plane, this feeling must first resound within the artist. Arm, hand, finger, the whole body, should be permeated by this feeling. Such devotion to work requires concentration and relaxation.

Brush drawing would never have reached the level shown here if the students had not prepared themselves through breathing, concentrating, and relaxing exercises.

Superficially fixed seeing, fluctuating thinking, and willful acting must give way to inner vision. This requires a readiness to be guided by inspiration. The painter must wait until his feeling urges him to create. In the moment of complete devotion all forms will be in the right relationship, as if they had created themselves. Nothing can be added or subtracted afterwards without alien and inorganic effect.

Every work created in this way surprises by its unforeseen formation. A famous Chinese ink picture consists of a single circle, painted on silk. To draw a large circle freehand with a brush requires complete control of the body and greatest concentration of the mind. Although this thin line is even all around, it is felt. One of the cardinal principles of the Chinese ink painter is "Heart and hand must be one."

The beginner becomes aware of the elastic point of the brush only when he really feels the form and is ready to follow this feeling. Brushes are superior to charcoal as expressive media because they permit richer nuances. Charcoal always produces the same dark stroke whether it is applied with a right or a left slant. But the brush allows rich variation. When the student has reached a certain sureness of movement and knows the difference between forms he has experienced and others he has not, he should be confronted with nature.

A pitcher is drawn in uninterrupted motion (Fig. 141). The form is right only when the three-dimensional pitcher, its hollow, its lip, the firmness of the handle and base, is drawn form genuine knowledge. A flower still life affords the opportunity for variously felt forms (Fig. 165). A human figure should be drawn only as far as it can be spontaneously represented by a deepened view of form. The motion of the hand follows the motion of the eye; as soon as seeing stops, drawing stops (Fig. 167).

A fern was studied for half an hour every morning during one week to learn to grasp and understand the movements of its characteristic form. On the last day the fern pot was put aside, and the drawing was produced in a single emotion within 15 minutes (Fig. 164).

Working with expressive forms yields new possibilities for the pictorial design of expressive themes like "Roaring Tiger," "Fighting Dogs," "Stampeding Horse" (Figs. 173, 174, 175). The manner of setting the theme is important. If I gave the assignment "The Tiger," the students would try to draw a decoratively striped animal. But when I say "The Roaring Tiger," the animal is in terrifying action. After the whole class tried to roar like a tiger, they imagined the danger of the beast.

Analyses of the works of the old masters also provide the opportunity for studies of feeling. When heart and hand are one during the designing of a form, this form becomes the bearer of intellectual-spiritual content. When we can relive this content from the form, we discover the effect of a work of art.

When I made the students at the Bauhaus analyze the weeping Magdalen by Grünewald, Oskar Schlemmer happened to be present. A letter to Otto Meyer-Amden of May 16th, 1921, in his book "Letters and Diaries" contains the following:

"Itten gives an 'analysis' in Weimar. He shows photographs after which the students are to draw the essentials; usually the movement, the main line, a curve. He refers them to a Gothic figure. Then he shows the weeping Magdalen from Grünewald's altar. The students try to distill something essential from this complex. Itten sees the attempts and thunders: 'If you had any artistic feeling you would not draw before this most exalted image of weeping, the weeping of the world, but you would sit here and melt into tears.'"

154 Attempts to represent the course of an emotion in a line. This exercise demands relaxation and involuntary "letting it happen."

155 Change and transition from plane feeling to line feeling.

156 Non-objective spot and line composition. Weimar, 1920. K. Auböck.

157 Flying Birds. Expressive composition which represents the motion of flying. This drawing was made in a lay class by a student of gymnastics. Berlin, 1928. S. Ludwig.

158 The band is strong and weak or heavy and light, drawn in swelling or diminishing uninterrupted motion. The rhythmic change between stressed and unstressed shows subjective feeling for proportion. Weimar, 1920.

159 A landscape painted with free emotion in spots and lines. Berlin, 1930. G. Pap.

160 Study of human figure expressed in light-dark tone values. Berlin, 1926. U. Klemm.

161 Lines intensified to spots and groups of spots. The drawing expressed a unified form-movement so that lines and spots appear to be related. Berlin, 1926.

162 Brush drawing of a branch from nature. It is considerably more difficult to observe and draw at the same time. The leaves are experienced as areas and painted as more or less dark spots without drawing outlines. Zurich, Textile Trade School, 1958.

163 To confront the students with new forms and proportions, I had them draw the most diverse plant forms. Here, a cactus is caught in a single powerful brush drawing. Berlin, 1932. S. Bauermeister.

164 The fern was intensively studied and drawn half an hour every morning for a week. On the last day I put the pot aside, and the students had 15 minutes to represent the fern. Study and observations had produced form imagination; it became deeper and more precise in the subconscious and could finally take shape. Berlin, 1930. I. Hirschlaff.

165 In the flower still life the forms of stems, leaves, and blossoms had to be translated into different motion forms and drawn in uninterrupted sequence. Berlin, 1928. Engeln-Hasbach.

160

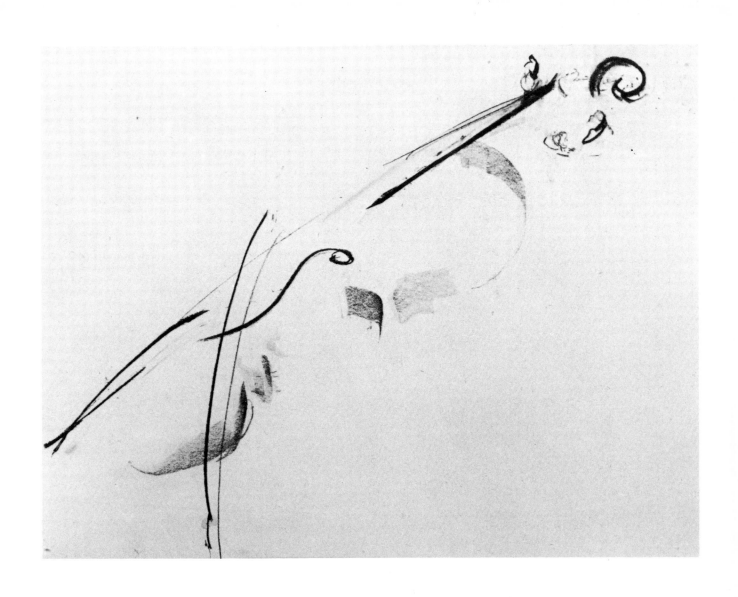

166 A kind of form-shorthand of a violin; it was drawn without previous study from nature to test the students' memory of the violin form. Berlin, 1928.

167 Portrait studies. Such exercises serve to synchronize eye and hand motion. When the eye ceases to observe, the hand stops to move. Only the spontaneously observed is produced in this way, not the previously known. Instantly experienced form relations are created instead of schematic designs of known details. Berlin, 1928.

168   The Friends. An attempt to capture the theme of friendship in line and tone relations. Berlin, 1928. A. Rehse.

169–170 Cats. Many fur and motion studies were made before this sensitive and vivid characterization of cats could be produced. Berlin, 1931. E. Kayser.

164

171 The sensitive design of Figs. 169 and 170 also appears in the self portrait with mirror and cat. I constantly advised the students to watch themselves in the mirror, to call themselves by their own names and to carry on dialogues with themselves. Berlin, 1931. E. Kayser.

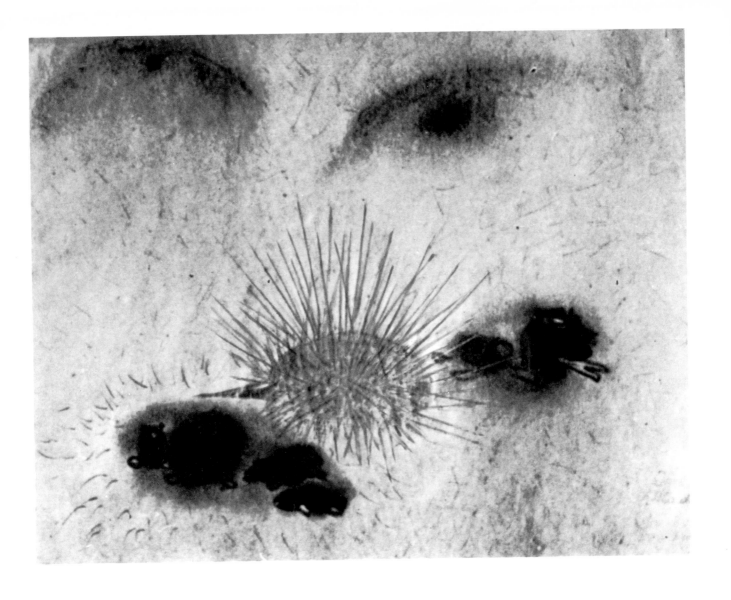

172 Hedgehog and mole. The hedgehog can be characterized by its long pointed quills. These quills must be drawn in an outward stabbing motion. The mole in its black velvety softness is a dark object in which only the little paws flash as light spots. The two animals are entirely different; this is here presented as contrast. Vienna, 1918.

166

173 Roaring Tiger. If the assignment is given as "The Tiger," all students would try to draw a decoratively striped animal. But when we say "The Tiger Roars," the animal is in terrifying action. After the whole class tried to roar like tigers, a mental image of the dangerous beast was produced. Even a jaguar trembles when the tiger roars. Berlin, 1928. B. von Graefe.

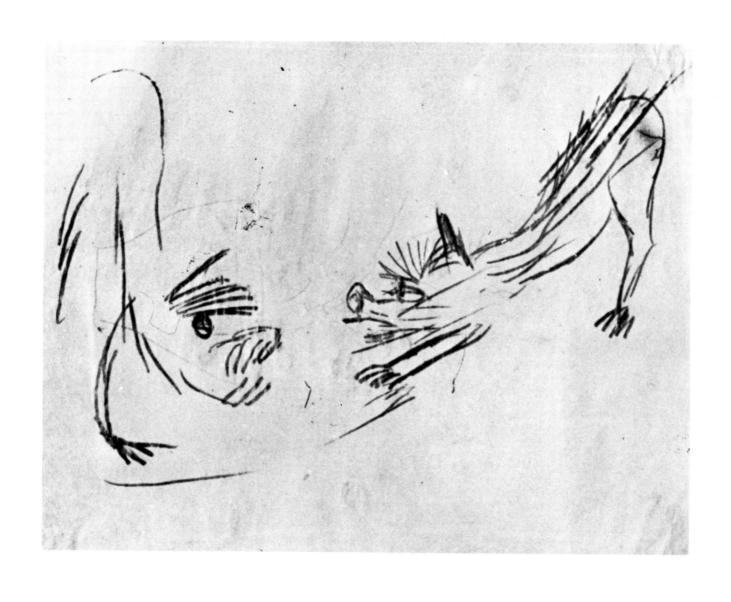

174 Quarrelling Dogs. In a few aggressive strokes the cowering, jealous curs yelp at each other. This expressive theme was drawn after an actual experience. Vienna, 1918. K. Auböck.

175 Stampede. A horse gallops wildly in enormous jumps. The helpless driver wrings his hands on the bucking, jolting wagon. The unanatomical form of the horse and the unreal suggestion of the wagon make this a scene of frightening expression. Vienna, 1919. O. Okuniewska.

176 The Outing. Well fed and content, father, mother, daughter, and dog are off on their Sunday outing from the city into the countryside. This original and humorous design was done as a month's assignment. Another solution of the same theme is reproduced in Fig. 25. The two illustrations show that independent homework on such a theme can further and express a student's genuine talent. Berlin, 1928. G. Itting.

177 At The Circus. The clown with blue suit, red nose, little yellow umbrella, and tiny elephant steps into the ring of the tent with the multicolored spectators in the stands. Berlin, 1928. G. Itting.

178 The Nightmare. What fright is conveyed here when we see the sleepwalker draw in his head and plunge down many stories. The ghostly white body is contrasted with the flickering textures in the windows. The designs "Outing," "Circus," and "Nightmare" (Figs. 176 – 178) were done by one student. He has succeeded to find the appropriate expressive forms and colors for each of these quite different themes. Berlin, 1928. G. Itting.

179 Gone Astray. A maze of infinite, undefinable paths represents a dreamlike experience. Such themes can inspire the student's imagination and capacity for experience. Krefeld, 1936. N. Diamantidi.

180 Analysis of a drawing of the weeping Magdalen by Mathias Grünewald. It does not seek an imitation of the drawing but a sensitive, expressive interpretation of weeping in linear elements.

174

181 Analysis of the "Crucifixion" by Grünewald. The analysis was to capture the tragedy of the event represented in the picture's light-dark and form characters.

182–183 Analyses of a Chinese ink painting. The dark spots of the feathers and the dark leaves in the branches have a relationship which characterizes the bird, safe in its hideaway.

In my Vienna painting class of 1918 I had a talented student of a most characteristic type. She was delicate, small, shy, and soft-spoken. Her eyes were like moonstones, and her pale skin was transparent. She wore her hair loose, and while she worked it sometimes fell over her face like a veil. Her drawings and watercolors were without lines, in gray tones as if veiled; they conformed exactly to the appearance of the artist.

This observation led me to recognize subjective forms and colors also in the works of other students. Simple people, unspoiled by schools, nearly always work in their subjective forms and colors. Where false instruction had destroyed the aptitude for original form, I found exercises which led the various students back to their appropriate forms.

The subjective character can appear in various ways: in the proportions, the form character, in light and dark, in lines, in textures, in colors, and often in combination of these means of expression.

There is a relationship between the shapes of man and the forms which he designs. The same forces which produce the specific shapes of a man according to his physical, spiritual, and intellectual constitution are able to influence the man's work. When a man is genuine, everything he does becomes a reflection of his own formative powers.

Fig. 184 illustrates the problem of these forces in a moving way. A curiously twisted figure sits on a cube, it seems unbalanced and lopsided. The student actually suffered from a hip ailment. All her drawings lacked balance until I pointed this out to her, and she was able to correct the fault rationally.

Another student never used tones in her compositions and drawings, always lines — crinkled and curly, if possible. She was blonde, fair-skinned, with strands of curling hair. Everything simple became complicated in her mind; she did not easily find her way in life (Figs. 185–186).

Figs. 187 and 188 represent a student with broad, large-scaled features, black hair and eyes. Her strong, simple, and large-scaled appearance is clearly reflected in the two designs which she made at the beginning of the first lesson.

The first goal of all teaching should be to develop genuine seeing, genuine feeling, and genuine thinking. Empty, superficial imitations should be removed like warts. Encouraging a return to original creativity frees the students from the constraint of mere outside learning. Every subjective form is genuine when it corresponds to the temperamental constitution of the artist.

I distinguish three basic types, the naturalistic-impressive, the intellectual-constructive, and the spiritual-expressive. Figs. 189 and 190 show a clear example of the naturalistic-impressive tendency. The drawing is the result of sharp visual observation and precise representation to the smallest details. The naturalistic-impressive type starts by observing the natural varieties and represents them realistically without expressive additions.

The intellectual-constructive type starts from the construction of an object and tries to grasp and geometrize everything clearly (Figs. 193, 194).

The spiritual-expressive type is guided by intuitive feelings; he neglects the constructive forms and studies the tone values with special care (Figs. 191 and 192). When we compare the two portraits, Figs. 192 and 194, we can easily see that these two students have entirely different temperaments. They worked side by side. One experienced the variety of light and dark tones emotionally; the other sought concise, clear, and constructively secure forms.

Figs. 193 and 195 show another pair of wholly different personalities. The roses (Fig. 195) are designed quite freely in tone values. The organic form relationship is dissolved into free emotional and expressive forms. In Fig. 193 the same roses are drawn in constructive, organic, and clearly geometrized forms.

In teaching drawing from nature I often gave the following assignment: Interpret the object first expressively, then constructively, then naturalistically, and finally in a generally valid design synthesis. Naturally, the student always succeeds best with the assignment which conforms to his own temperament. Such exercises shed a clear light on the strong and weak points of each constitution. Through his reason, man is able to recognize the impersonal principle and to use it objectively. In a deeper sense, all measuring and constructing is a method to overcome personal limitations and shortcomings and to arrive at an objective and generally valid statement.

When dealing with subjective colors or subjective forms, it is valuable for teachers and artists to know and consider these facts. Such study leads us to recognize our own powers and to respect the other-ness of our fellow men.

Teachers should be careful not to urge their own forms and colors on the students. Every student's own subjective gifts should be unlocked. The objective principles of form and color help the student to strengthen his own powers and to expand his creative talent.

184 This unbalanced figure was drawn by a student who suffered from a hip ailment. Berlin, 1928.

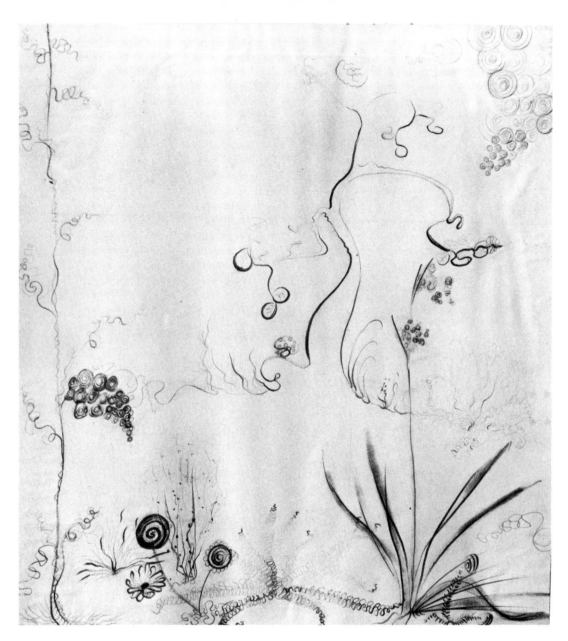

185 – 186 All free compositions of this student emphasized line, and the curly forms matched her hair. Berlin, 1930.

187 – 188 The large black forms of this proportion study in light-dark, a first assignment, reflect the simple large-scaled features of the student. Berlin, 1931.

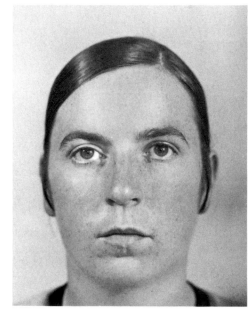

189 – 190 Realistically detailed nature study of an impressive temperament. Sharp observation and exact representation of many natural details
are characteristic for this type. Only felt or only constructed forms would
be unsatisfying for this student. Berlin, 1928.

191 – 192 After a short time this student found the world of tones which conformed to her spiritual-expressive temperament. If a teacher of constructive constitution had given her only constructive themes, she would soon have been one of the most untalented students. Berlin, 1926.

193–194 This simple type of design, stressing the constructive and showing the organic, corresponds to the student's simple, rational, straightforward way of thinking. Berlin, 1926.

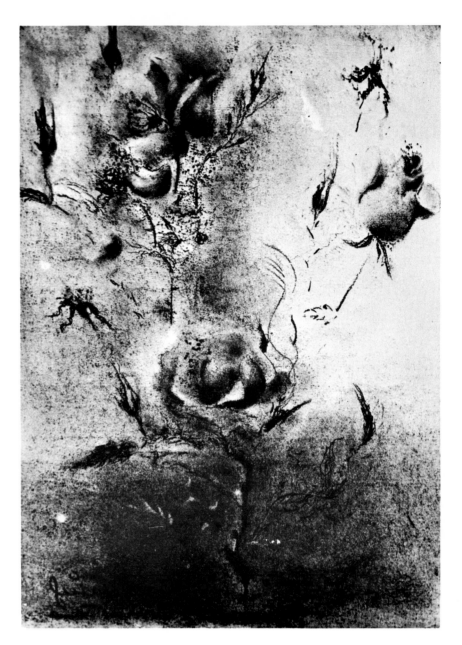

195 – 196 The student's emotional expression suggests an expressive temperament. The organic form of the roses was decomposed in favor of expression and dissolved in a tonal image. This is a drawing of the same roses shown in Fig. 193, done at the same time. The different temperamental and constitutional conceptions of a theme are here clearly apparent. Berlin, 1926.

197 Common drawing exercises in class before starting individual work. Berlin, 1930.

I thank Messrs. Karl Maier and Otto Julius Maier for their spontaneous readiness to publish this book and for all the publisher's efforts to meet my suggestions in the design of the book.

The illustrations are reproduced from originals by students; I would like to express my special gratitude to the students here. I regret that it was not possible to find the names of all the students who produced illustrations. The illustrative material is also not without gaps, and it does not always show the best solutions of an assignment.

I owe the finding of so many works to the tireless search, photography and collaboration of my wife. They have suffered in the course of many years, and this cannot be hidden in good reproduction.

I should like to thank the Bauhaus Archive in Darmstadt for the photos for the illustrations 38, 69, 143, 144 and 149.

If this book can guide, encourage and stimulate other students and young artists on their hard road, my wish will be fulfilled.

Zurich, July 12th, 1963   Johannes Itten

Page numbers of illustrations are set in **bold face**.